FROM COLUMBUS TO COLONIAL AMERICA

1492 to 1763

FROM COLUMBUS TO COLONIAL AMERICA
1492 to 1763

EDITED BY JEFF WALLENFELDT, MANAGER, GEOGRAPHY AND HISTORY

Britannica®
Educational Publishing

IN ASSOCIATION WITH

ROSEN
EDUCATIONAL SERVICES

Published in 2012 by Britannica Educational Publishing
(a trademark of Encyclopædia Britannica, Inc.)
in association with Rosen Educational Services, LLC
29 East 21st Street, New York, NY 10010.

Distributed exclusively by Rosen Educational Services.
For a listing of additional Britannica Educational Publishing titles, call toll free (800) 237-9932.

First Edition

Britannica Educational Publishing
Michael I. Levy: Executive Editor
Marilyn L. Barton: Senior Coordinator, Production Control
Steven Bosco: Director, Editorial Technologies
Lisa S. Braucher: Senior Producer and Data Editor
Yvette Charboneau: Senior Copy Editor
Kathy Nakamura: Manager, Media Acquisition
Jeff Wallenfeldt: Manager, Geography and History

Rosen Educational Services
Jeanne Nagle: Senior Editor
Nelson Sá: Art Director
Cindy Reiman: Photography Manager
Karen Huang: Photo Researcher
Matthew Cauli: Cover Design
Brian Garvey: Designer
Introduction by Jeff Wallenfeldt

Library of Congress Cataloging-in-Publication Data

From Columbus to colonial America: 1492 to 1763/edited by Jeff Wallenfeldt.—1st ed.
    p. cm.—(Documenting America: the primary source documents of a nation)
"In association with Britannica Educational Publishing, Rosen Educational Services."
Includes bibliographical references and index.
ISBN 978-1-61530-662-6 (library binding)
[1. United States—History—Colonial period, ca. 1600–1775. 2. United States—History—Colonial period, ca. 1600–1775—Sources.] I. Wallenfeldt, Jeffrey H.
E188.F76 2012
973.2—dc22

2011016194

Manufactured in the United States of America

On the cover: Early settlers carry lumber and raise the walls of the stockade fort at Jamestown, Va., the first permanent English settlement in America. *Hulton Archive/Getty Images*. A letter from Christopher Columbus. *Hulton Archive/Getty Images*

On page viii-ix: Columbus arriving on the shores of the New World. *Library of Congress Prints and Photographs Division*

On pages 1, 10, 35, 46, 59 , 64: Jamestown settlers load barrels of tobacco on a ship for export. Tobacco was the mainstay crop in Virginia, upon which the colony's economy was built. *MPI/ Archive Photos/Getty Images*

CONTENTS

2

17

37

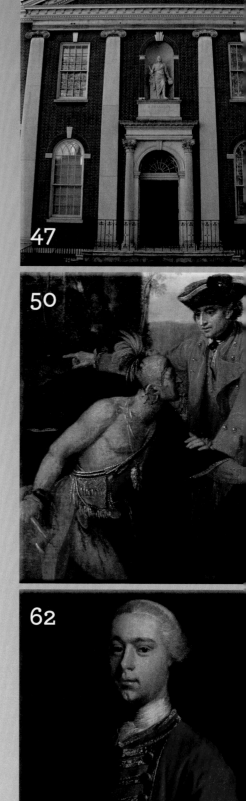

47

50

62

65

Depending on who is doing the telling, the story of the United States of America is revolutionary and reactionary, romantic and rational, drenched in myth and stripped down to cold, hard facts. There is to be much said for narrative history fashioned at the remove of time. Generally there is a consistency of approach, a clarity of meaning, and a momentum to the telling. Things get messier when the story is related by participants or described in the moment as events unfold. The stakes are usually higher in primary source accounts, emotions closer to the surface, and agendas more naked.

This volume attempts to present the best of both approaches. Interweaving primary source accounts into a narrative history fuses scholarly insight (and the advantage of hindsight) with the passion of immediacy to fully document the American experience. When they are brief enough, these primary source documents are presented in their entirety in running text. More often, a brief characteristic excerpt offers a flavor of the fuller document found in the appendix. All of the documents are prefaced by introductions that provide further context.

The canvas on which American history has unfolded is a sprawling continent teeming with fertile land and natural resources, a land of woodlands and prairies, lakes great and small, mountains and plains, deserts and swamps. Yet until the 15th century, this land was an unknown entity, at least to European civilizations (with the possible exception of a few intrepid Vikings). For them it was the New World—even though it was already populated, albeit rather sparsely, by indigenous peoples. These Native Americans mostly called themselves "the People," but they would become known as Indians because the first European "discoverers" of the New World had been seeking a shorter route to Cathay (China) and India and were convinced that they had succeeded.

Traditionally, the study of U.S. history has begun not with the Americas' rich indigenous cultures but with the out-of-the-ocean-blue arrival of Christopher Columbus in 1492. He had come in search of the bounties of Asia, and he returned with enough of the sought-after spices and gold to convince his royal Spanish sponsors that exaggerated accounts of his discoveries merited the outfitting even greater expeditions. He came back baring colourful parrots as evidence of the exotic world he had encountered. He brought back human specimens as well—Indians, whose generosity he described in a letter to another of his patrons, Lord Sanchez, but whom his men had brutally captured. Columbus's pledge to exploit the gold and spices of the New World for the glory of the Spanish empire was accompanied by a promise to procure "as many men for service of the navy as Their Majesties may require."

Throughout the century following Columbus's voyages, the Spanish dominated European competition for the Americas. Yet the English navy's defeat of the Spanish Armada in 1588 helped open the way to English settlement in the New World. In 1607 three ships brought some 100 colonists to Virginia, the name the English used for the entire East Coast of North America north of present-day Florida. On a peninsula at the mouth of the James River (in the modern-day state of Virginia) the Virginia Company of London established the privately financed Jamestown colony. Colonists came intent on finding gold, silver, and a river route to Asia, but they also came at a time when there was a fascination with stories of a lush, rustic dream world free from the complexity and corruption of city life. Pastoral literature dated back even farther than ancient Roman poet Virgil's accounts of shepherds in the idyllic green fields of Arcadia, but it reached new heights in the late 16th century poems of Edmund Spenser. His patron, Sir Philip Sidney, not only wrote his own *Arcadia*, but also financed the expeditions of explorer Martin Frobisher, dreamed of sailing with Sir Walter Raleigh, and longed to establish a colony in Virginia

The New World described by John Smith, one of the leaders of Jamestown, in his *Generall Historie of Virginia*, was exotic and full of adventure but far from idyllic. Whether Smith's famous account of his rescue from death at the hands of the Powhattan Indians through the intervention of a chief's daughter, Pochahantas,, is self-aggrandizing fiction, a misinterpretation of events, or documentary truth, the *Historie* paints a vivid picture of a struggle for survival in often an harsh environment. Half of all Jamestown colonists died within the first year from sickness and starvation. Their extreme circumstances were never clearer than in Smith's description of one colonist who was executed for eating "powdered wife."

English settlement of North America continued elsewhere. Just before landing in Plymouth (in modern-day Massachusetts) in 1620, the Pilgrims, members of the English Separatist Church who were seeking religious freedom, pledged themselves to cooperative effort in the Mayflower Compact. *Of Plymouth Plantation*, the history of the colony's first decades written by its second governor, William Bradford, details a "starving time" much like that experienced by the denizens of Jamestown, a period when many colonists perished and the selfless efforts of a heroic few kept the colony going. Bradford chronicles the evolution of the Pilgrims' approach to communal responsibility; mutual support remained crucial, but they also found that more life-sustaining corn was cultivated when individuals grew the bulk of it for their own families rather than for the community. *Of Plymouth Plantation* is also the story of negotiation, cooperation, and détente between Plymouth colony and Native Americans.

Despite its plucky triumph in sustaining its community, Plymouth Colony was, by 1691, absorbed by the larger Massachusetts Bay colony. Founded by the less religiously radical Puritans, who sought to "purify" rather than desert the Church of England, the Bay colony grew around Boston. The duties its citizens to their government were carefully defined in 1634 in *The Oath of a Freeman*. The church-centered government that developed under governor John Winthrop not only limited the vote to church members, but produced a relatively rigid society in which dissent sometimes led to expulsion or emigration. The Bay colony's most famous dissenter, Roger Williams, left to found Providence, whose greater toleration was evidenced in its *Plan for Civil Government*.

Among the colonies that constituted English North America, Maryland became a bastion of Roman Catholicism. Pennsylvania, one of the most tolerant and diverse colonies, was founded by William Penn and other members of the Society of Friends, whose belief that there was a divine spirit in all people was articulated by Penn in *The People Called Quakers*. Penn grounded his "experiment in the New World" on his belief in the principles of liberty of conscience and pacifism. Farther south, James

Oglethorpe brought imprisoned debtors from England to Georgia for a new start. King Charles II granted ownership of Carolinas to a number of his friends, who advertised for settlers with a pamphlet that not only trumpeted the colony's bountiful land and "wholesome air" but promised free land for freemen and freewomen, and even for indentured servants after their period of service.

As it became clear that raising crops for export rather than subsistence was the way to success in the American colonies, tobacco became the staple of the economies of Virginia and Maryland, while the Mid-Atlantic states turned principally to growing grains. In New England, trade, fishing, and craftsmanship dominated. The tradition of the town meeting broadened political involvement in New England, but there, as elsewhere in the colonies, political and economic power remained concentrated in the hands of relatively few privileged men. Through legislation such as the Navigation Act of 1660, the British crown tightened its hold on trade within its colonies. Its control of colonial politics was more tenuous, and local governments grew stronger.

By 1760 the colonial population of British America had swelled from little more than 50,000 in 1650 to some 1.7 million people. Initially the settlers had been primarily English, but by the early 18th century, Germans, Irish, and Scots-Irish also had begun to immigrate in large numbers. The most dramatic increase was in the number of Africans brought involuntarily as a slaves. The black population of South Carolina, for example, went from about 2,500 in 1700 to more than 80,000 in 1760. Despite the Carolina pamphlet's promise of a deferred payoff for indentured servants, indentured servitude for blacks gave way to lifelong chattel slavery. In a letter to his brother in 1757, the Rev. Peter Fontaine of Virginia offers a disturbing rationalization of the enslavement of blacks at a time when the institution of slavery was becoming the bedrock of the southern economy.

Early colonial America's most notable contributions to the arts and sciences came in the field of applied science, as the challenge of taming the land gave rise to ingenuity. Benjamin Franklin, in particular, is noted for his pioneering experiments with electricity and his invention of a slew of practical devices—from bifocals to a wood-burning stove. Franklin was also an elegant writer. Some of his finest pieces, such as "The Speech of Polly Baker," from 1747, appeared in newspapers, as did much of the most important writing in America. Among the other notable contributions to early American literature are the colonial histories written by Robert Beverly and William Byrd in the early 18th century, which are as evocative and entertaining as they are informative. Additionally, the establishment of quality institutions of higher education also became a priority of colonial cultural life, as is reflected in John Eliot's appeal for sponsorship of the fledging college that would become Harvard University.

As the 17th century gave way to the 18th century, colonial life and government became more secular. Religion, however, remained central to the American experience even as it became more diversified with the influx of adherents to different faiths, from Catholicism and Anabaptism to Judaism. Still, the Puritans' conviction that they had a special covenant with God to establish a model society in the New World, as an example for all, remained a powerful idea. Massachusetts governor John Winthrop's description of this call for American exceptionalism, expressed as the duty to build "City on a Hill," would echo throughout American history, from Peter Bulkeley's mid-17th century sermon "The Gospel-Covenant" to the rhetoric of Pres. Ronald Reagan in late 20th century. In the 1730s and '40s, a religious revival known as the Great Awakening reinvigorated religious life in America, as fire-and-brimstone preachers excited new commitments to faith with promises of salvation and threats of damnation. Jonathan Edwards, one of the movement's most influential figures, best remembered for his warning to "Sinners in the Hands of Angry God," described the Great Awakening in a letter of 1743 to fellow minister Thomas Prince, in which he began to question the sincerity of some converts.

Before long the spiritual battle for colonial souls took a back seat to the physical battle for control of North America. The Great War for Empire (also called the French and Indian War) was the latest chapter in an ongoing power struggle among, Britain, France, and the other great European empires; it was fought at sea and on land in more than one continent. In North America both the French and the British enlisted the aid of Native Americans. When the fighting was over—with France defeated and Canada, Florida, and all territory east of the Mississippi ceded to Britain—the Indians were no longer able to play one colonial power off against the other. Some colonists, such as Puritan leader Sam Sewall, had sought to treat the Native Americans fairly, but most did not. As the colonists began to covet and converge upon lands farther into the interior of the continent, the Indian defense of their lands escalated.

As the Great War for Empire ended, the colonists were ever more self-sufficient, self-governing, and self-aware. They also were many steps closer toward the freedom and democracy that had been welling on the edges of their consciousness all along.

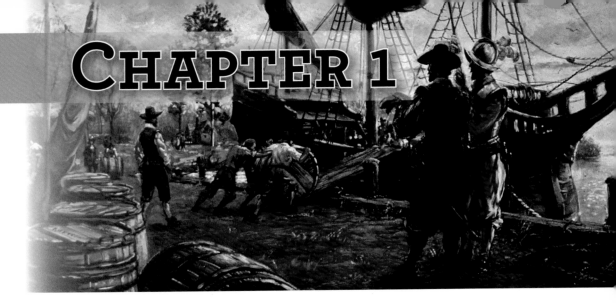

CHAPTER 1

A NEW WORLD

On Aug. 3, 1492, Christopher Columbus sailed from Palos, Spain, with three small ships manned by Spaniards. From the Canary Islands he sailed westward, for, on the evidence of the globes and maps in which he had faith, Japan was on the same latitude. If Japan should be missed, Columbus thought that the route adopted would land him, only a little further on, off the coast of China itself. Fair winds favoured him and the sea was calm. On October 12, Columbus made landfall on the Bahamaian island of Guanahaní, which he renamed San Salvador. With the help of the local Indians, the ships reached Cuba and then Haiti. Although there was no sign of the wealth of the lands of Kublai Khan, Columbus nevertheless seemed convinced that he had reached China since, according to his reckoning, he was beyond Japan.

Whatever Columbus thought, it was clear to others that there was much to be investigated, and probably much to be gained, by exploration westward. Not only in Lisbon and Cádiz but also in other Atlantic ports, groups of men congregated in hopes of joining in the search. In May 1497, John Cabot set out from Bristol, Eng., with one small ship, the *Matthew*, taking a course due west from Dursey Head,

An illustration showing Christopher Columbus and his fleet in Spain, setting sail for the New World on August 3, 1492. Kean Collection/Archive Photos/Getty Images

Ireland. His landfall on the other side of the ocean was probably on the northern peninsula of the island now known as Newfoundland. From there, Cabot explored southward. Little is known of his first voyage, and almost nothing of his second, in 1498, from which he did not return, but his voyages in high latitudes represented almost as great a navigational feat as those of Columbus. Like those earlier voyages, Cabot's journeys paved the way for further exploration that would eventually result in European settlement of North America.

BEFORE COLUMBUS

The territory represented by the continental United States had, of course, been discovered, perhaps several times, before the voyages of Columbus. When Columbus arrived, he found the New World inhabited by peoples who in all likelihood had originally come from the continent of Asia. Probably these first inhabitants had arrived 20,000 to 35,000 years before in a series of migrations from Asia to North America by way of the Bering Strait. By the time the first Europeans appeared, the indigenous (or first) people, commonly referred to as Indians, had spread and occupied all portions of the New World.

The foods and other resources available in each region of the land largely determined the type of culture that existed there. Fish and sea mammals, for example, contributed the bulk of the food supply of coastal peoples, although the acorn was a staple for California Indians. Plant life and wild game (especially the American bison, or buffalo) were food sources for the Plains Indians, while small-game hunting and fishing (again, depending on local resources) provided for Midwestern and Eastern American Indian groups. These foods were supplemented by corn, which the Indians called "maize." This was a staple food for the Indians of the Southwest. Native Americans depended on fishing, hunting, plant and berry gathering, and special farming techniques to get food, depending on what type of sustenance was available in a given area.

Food and other raw materials likewise had an effect on the groups' material culture—that is, on the things they owned and how they used them. All Indians transported goods by human carrier, although the use of dogs to pull sleds or travois was widespread. Rafts, boats, and canoes were used where water facilities were available. The horse, imported by the Spanish in the early 16th century, was quickly adopted by the American Indians once it had made its appearance. Notably, horses came to be used widely by the buffalo-hunting Indians of the Great Plains.

American Indian culture groups were distinguished, among other ways, by house types. Dome-shaped ice houses (igloos) were developed by the Eskimos (called the Inuit in Canada) in what would become Alaska. Rectangular plank houses were produced by the Northwest Coast Indians, while Plains and Prairie tribes lived in lodges and tepees made

Native Americans of the 16th century paddle a canoe full of surplus crops destined for a riverside storehouse. Three Lions/Hulton Archive/Getty Images

from dirt and animal skins. The Pueblo Indians of the American Southwest are known for building flat-roofed and often multistoried houses. The Northeast Indians lived in barrel houses. Clothing, or the lack of it, likewise varied with native groups, as did crafts, weapons, and tribal economic, social, and religious customs.

At the time of Columbus's arrival there were roughly 1.5 million American Indians in what is now the continental United States, although estimates vary greatly. In order to determine the role and impact of American Indians upon the subsequent history of the United States in any meaningful way, one must understand the various factors that made Native American tribes different from one another, such as those mentioned above. Generally speaking, however, it may be said that the American Indians as a whole exercised an important influence upon the civilization transplanted from Europe to the New World. Indian foods and herbs, manufactured tools and other

Document: Christopher Columbus: Discovery of the New World (1493)

The story of America's "discovery" by Christopher Columbus is familiar to every schoolchild, yet neither Christopher Columbus nor any of his crew realized what it was they had discovered. On the first of his four voyages to the New World, Christopher Columbus led a flotilla of three ships, the Niña, the Pinta, and his flagship, the Santa Maria, that departed from Palos, Spain, in the summer of 1492 and arrived in the Bahamas in October of that year. (Land was sighted for the first time at dawn on October 12.) The expedition touched at such Caribbean islands as San Salvador, Cuba, and Española (Santo Domingo).

Convinced that he had discovered "the Indies," Columbus established trading posts and returned to Spain to announce his success and organize a larger expedition. He stopped at Lisbon on his way home, and from there sent a description of the lands and people he had seen to Lord Raphael Sanchez, treasurer of Aragon and one of his patrons. In the letter, dated March 14, 1493, Columbus referred to the natives he had found as "Indians," believing, as he did until his death, that he had reached the eastern shores of Asia.

Knowing that it will afford you pleasure to learn that I have brought my undertaking to a successful termination, I have decided upon writing you this letter to acquaint you with all the events which have occurred in my voyage, and the discoveries which have resulted from it. Thirty-three days after my departure from [Gomera] I reached the Indian Sea, where I discovered many islands, thickly peopled, of which I took possession without resistance in the name of our most illustrious monarch, by public proclamation and with unfurled banners. To the first of these islands, which is called by the Indians Guanahani, I gave the name of the blessed Savior (San Salvador), relying upon whose protection I had reached this as well as the other islands; to each of these I also gave a name, ordering that one should be called Santa Maria de la Concepcion, another Fernandina, the third Isabella, the fourth Juana [Cuba], and so with all the rest....

As soon as we arrived at that, which as I have said was named Juana, I proceeded along its coast a short distance westward and found it to be so large and apparently without termination that I could not suppose it to be an island, but the continental province of Cathay. Seeing, however, no towns or populous places on the seacoast, but only a few detached houses and cottages, with whose inhabitants I was unable to communicate because they fled as soon as they saw us, I went further on, thinking that in my progress I should certainly find some city or village....

articles, methods of raising some crops, war techniques, words and folklore, and ethnic infusions are among the more obvious general contributions of the Indians to European settlement culture.

THE EUROPEAN BACKGROUND

The English colonization of North America was but one chapter in the larger story of European expansion throughout the globe. The Portuguese, beginning with a voyage to Porto Santo off the coast of West Africa in 1418, were the first Europeans to promote overseas exploration and colonization. By 1487 the Portuguese had traveled all the way to the southern tip of Africa, establishing trading stations at Arguin, Sierra Leone, and El Mina. In 1497 Vasco da Gama rounded the Cape of Good Hope and sailed up the eastern coast of Africa, laying the groundwork for Portugal's later commercial control of India. By 1500, when Pedro Álvares Cabral stumbled across the coast of Brazil en route to India, Portuguese

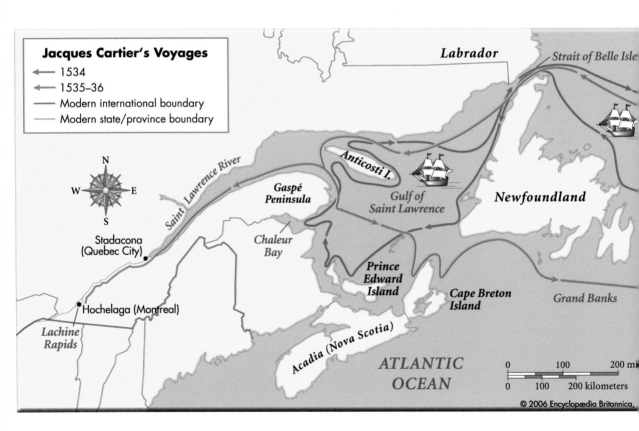

Jacques Cartier's Voyages

← 1534
← 1535–36
— Modern international boundary
— Modern state/province boundary

Labrador

Strait of Belle Isle

Saint Lawrence River

Anticosti I.

Gaspé Peninsula

Gulf of Saint Lawrence

Newfoundland

Stadacona (Quebec City)

Chaleur Bay

Prince Edward Island

Cape Breton Island

Grand Banks

Hochelaga (Montreal)

Lachine Rapids

Acadia (Nova Scotia)

ATLANTIC OCEAN

N W E S

0   100   200 mi
0   100   200 kilometers

© 2006 Encyclopædia Britannica, Inc.

influence had expanded to the New World as well.

Though initially lagging behind the Portuguese in the arts of navigation and exploration, the Spanish quickly closed that gap in the decades following Columbus's voyages to America. First in the Caribbean and then in spectacular conquests of New Spain and Peru, they captured the imagination, and the envy, of the European world.

France, occupied with wars in Europe to preserve its own territorial integrity, was not able to devote as much time or effort to overseas expansion as did Spain and Portugal. Beginning in the early 16th century, however, French fishermen established an outpost in Newfoundland, and in 1534 Jacques Cartier began exploring the Gulf of St. Lawrence. By 1543 the French had ceased their efforts to colonize the northeast portion of the New World. In the last half of the 16th century, France attempted to found colonies in Florida and Brazil, but each of these efforts failed, and by the end of the century Spain and Portugal remained the only two European nations to have established successful colonies in America.

ENGLISH COLONIZATION

The English, although eager to duplicate the Spanish and Portuguese successes, nevertheless lagged far behind in their colonization efforts. The English possessed a theoretical claim to the North American mainland by dint of Cabot's 1497 voyage, but in fact they had neither the means nor the desire to back up that claim during the 16th century. Thus it was that England relied instead on private trading companies, which were interested principally in commercial rather than territorial expansion, to defend its interests in the expanding European world.

The first of these commercial ventures began with the formation of the Muscovy Company in 1554. In 1576–78 the English mariner Martin Frobisher undertook three voyages in search of a Northwest Passage to the Far East. In 1577 Sir Francis Drake made his famous voyage around the world, plundering the western coast of South America en route. A year later Sir Humphrey Gilbert, one of the most dedicated of Elizabethan imperialists, began a series of ventures aimed at establishing permanent colonies in North America. All his efforts met with what was, at best, limited success. Finally, in September 1583, Gilbert, with five vessels and 260 men, disappeared in the North Atlantic.

With the failure of Gilbert's voyage, the English turned to a new man, Sir Walter Raleigh, and a new strategy—a southern rather than a northern route to North America—to advance England's fortunes in the New World. Although Raleigh's efforts to found a permanent colony off the coast of North Carolina did finally fail with the mysterious destruction of the Roanoke Island colony in 1587, they awakened popular interest in a permanent colonizing venture.

A colourized portrait of Sir Walter Raleigh, the British explorer who founded a colony in present-day North Carolina yet never set foot there himself. Stock Montage/Archive Photos/Getty Images

During the years separating the failure of the Roanoke attempt and the establishment in 1607 of Jamestown colony, English propagandists worked hard to convince the public that a settlement in America would yield instant and easily exploitable wealth. Even men such as the English geographer Richard Hakluyt were not certain that the Spanish colonization experience could or should be imitated but hoped nevertheless that the English colonies in the New World would prove to be a source of immediate commercial gain. There were, of course, other motives for colonization. Some hoped to discover the much-sought-after route to the Orient (East Asia) in North America. English imperialists thought it necessary to settle in the New World in order to limit Spanish expansion.

CHAPTER 2

SETTLEMENT

Once it was proved that America was a suitable place for settlement, some Englishmen would travel to those particular colonies that promised to free them from religious persecution. There were also Englishmen, primarily of lower- and middle-class origin, who hoped the New World would provide them with increased economic opportunity in the form of free or inexpensive land. While these two motives have been given considerable attention by historians, they appear not to have been so much original motives for English colonization as they were shifts of attitude once colonization had begun.

VIRGINIA

The leaders of the Virginia Company, a joint-stock company in charge of the Jamestown enterprise, were for the most part wealthy and wellborn commercial and military adventurers eager to find new outlets for investment. During the first two years of its existence, the Virginia colony, under the charter of 1607, proved an extraordinarily bad investment. This was principally due to the unwillingness of the early colonizers

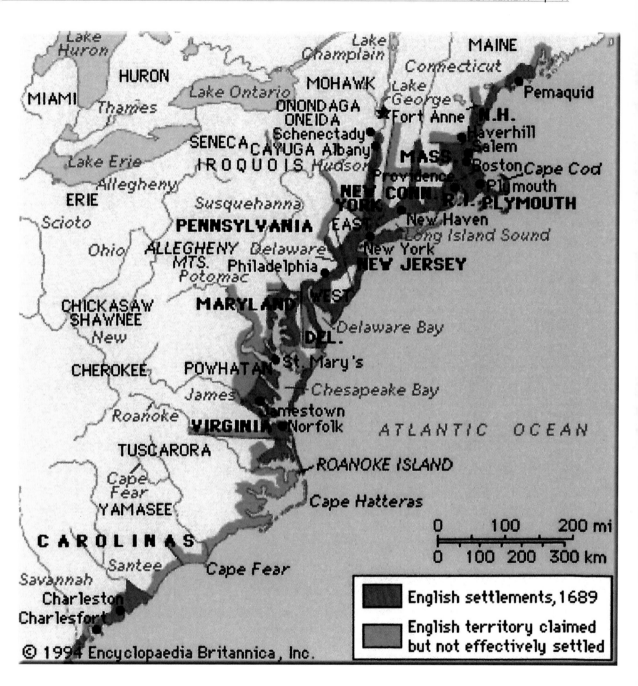

English colonies in 17th-century North America, with locations of Native American peoples.

to do the necessary work of providing for themselves and to the chronic shortage of capital to supply the venture.

A new charter in 1609 significantly broadened membership in the Virginia Company, thereby temporarily increasing the supply of capital at the disposal of its directors. Yet most of the settlers continued to act as though they expected the American Indians to provide for their existence, a notion that the Indians fiercely rejected. As a result, the enterprise still failed to yield any profits, and the number of investors again declined.

The crown issued a third charter in 1612, authorizing the company to institute a lottery to raise more capital for the floundering enterprise. In that same year, John Rolfe harvested the first crop of a high-grade, and therefore potentially profitable, strain of tobacco. At about the same time, with the arrival of Sir Thomas Dale in the colony as governor in 1611, the settlers gradually began to practice the discipline necessary for their survival, though at an enormous personal cost.

Dale carried with him the "Laws Divine, Morall, and Martial," which were intended to supervise nearly every aspect of the settlers' lives. Each person in Virginia, including women and children, was given a military rank, with duties spelled out in minute detail. Penalties imposed for violating these rules were severe. Those who failed to obey the work regulations were to be forced to lie with neck and heels together all night for the first offense, whipped for the second, and sent to a year's service in English galleys

(convict ships) for the third. The settlers could hardly protest the harshness of the code, for that might be deemed slander against the company—an offense punishable by service in the galleys or by death.

Dale's code brought order to the Virginia experiment, but it hardly served to attract new settlers. To increase incentive the company, beginning in 1618, offered 50 acres (about 20 hectares) of land to those settlers who could pay their transportation to Virginia and a promise of 50 acres after seven years of service to those who could not pay their passage. Concurrently, the new governor of Virginia, Sir George Yeardley, issued a call for the election of representatives to a House of Burgesses, which was to convene in Jamestown in July 1619. In its original form the House of Burgesses was little more than an agency of the governing board of the Virginia Company, but it would later expand its powers and prerogatives and become an important force for colonial self-government.

Despite the introduction of these reforms, the years from 1619 to 1624 proved fatal to the future of the Virginia Company. Epidemics, constant warfare with the Indians, and internal disputes took a heavy toll on the colony. In 1624 the crown finally revoked the charter of the company and placed the colony under royal control. The introduction of royal government into Virginia, while it was to have important long-range consequences, did not produce an immediate change in the character of the colony. The economic and political life of the colony

Document: John Smith: Starving Time in Virginia (1607–14)

In December 1606, the Virginia Company sent three ships to Virginia with 144 colonists, only 105 of whom actually disembarked at Jamestown the following May. Among them was Capt. John Smith, a soldier-adventurer and promoter of the company, who became its chief historian. He had an especially resourceful spirit in many a dark day, and he saved the colony from starvation during the winter of 1608–09 by obtaining corn from the Indians he had befriended. On an expedition to discover the source of the Chickahominy River, Captain Smith was captured by the Indians and was to be executed. As the controversial legend holds, Pocahontas saved his life by throwing herself upon him and entreating her father, Powhatan, to spare Smith.

Smith's Generall Historie of Virginia, *an indispensable—though at times unreliable—work, is reprinted here in part. The selection deals with the events of 1607-14 and is actually a series of reports or accounts by various persons with interpolations by Smith himself. Thus, part of the narrative covers an interval when he had returned temporarily to England.*

1607. Being thus left to our fortunes, it fortuned that within ten days scarce ten among us could either go or well stand, such extreme weakness and sickness oppressed us. And thereat none need marvel if they consider the cause and reason, which was this.

While the ships stayed, our allowance was somewhat bettered by a daily proportion of biscuits, which the sailors would pilfer to sell, give, or exchange with us for money, sassafras, furs, or love. But when they departed, there remained neither tavern, beer, house, nor place of relief, but the common kettle. Had we been as free from all sins as gluttony and drunkenness, we might have been canonized for saints; but our president [Wingfield] would never have been admitted for engrossing to his private [use] oatmeal, sack, aquavitae, beef, eggs, or what not, but the kettle; that indeed he allowed equally to be distributed, and that was half a pint of wheat, and as much barley boiled with water for a man a day, and this having

George Percy, governor of the Jamestown Colony during the Starving Time, engraving.

fried some twenty-six weeks in the ship's hold, contained as many worms as grains; so that we might truly call it rather so much bran than corn, our drink was water, our lodgings castles in the air.

With this lodging and diet, our extreme toil in bearing and planting palisades so strained and bruised us, and our continual labor in the extremity of the heat had so weakened us, as were cause sufficient to have made us as miserable in our native country, or any other place in the world...

continued as it had in the past. Though its future under the royal commission of 1624 was uncertain, the House of Burgesses continued to meet on an informal basis; by 1629 it had been officially reestablished. The crown also grudgingly acquiesced to the decision of the Virginia settlers to continue to direct most of their energies to the growth and exportation of tobacco. By 1630 the Virginia colony, while not prosperous, at least was showing signs that it was capable of surviving without royal subsidy.

MARYLAND

Maryland, Virginia's neighbour to the north, was the first English colony to be controlled by a single proprietor rather than by a joint-stock company. Lord Baltimore (George Calvert) had been an investor in a number of colonizing schemes before being given a grant of land from the crown in 1632. Baltimore was given a sizable grant of power to go along with his grant of land; he had control over the trade and political system of the colony so long as he did nothing to deviate from the laws of England.

Baltimore's son Cecilius Calvert, the second Lord Baltimore, took over the project at his father's death and promoted a settlement at St. Mary's on the Potomac. Supplied in part by Virginia, the Maryland colonists managed to sustain their settlement in modest fashion from the beginning. As in Virginia, however, the early 17th-century settlement in Maryland was often unstable and unrefined. Composed overwhelmingly of young single males—many of them indentured servants—it lacked the stabilizing force of a strong family structure to temper the rigours of life in the wilderness.

The colony was intended to serve at least two purposes. Baltimore, a Roman Catholic, was eager to found a colony where Catholics could live in peace, but he was also eager to see his colony yield him as large a profit as possible. From the outset, Protestants outnumbered Catholics, although a few prominent Catholics tended to own an inordinate share of the land in the colony. Despite this favouritism in the area of land policy, Baltimore was for the most part a good and fair administrator.

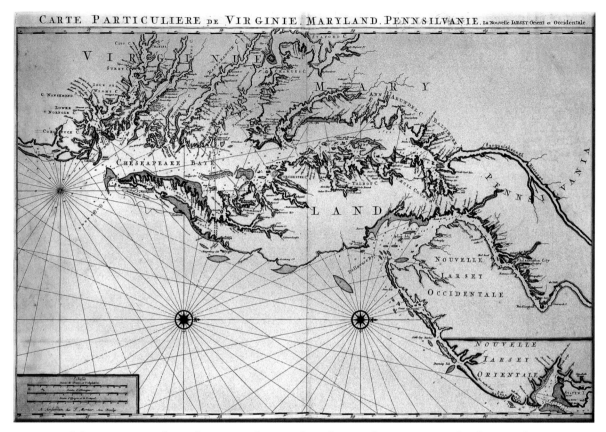

French-language map from about 1700 showing the colonies of Virginia, Maryland, Pennsylvania, and New Jersey. Library of Congress, Washington, D.C.

Following the accession of William III and Mary II to the English throne, however, control of the colony was taken away from the Calvert family and entrusted to the royal government. Shortly thereafter, the crown decreed that Anglicanism would be the established religion of the colony. In 1715, after the Calvert family had renounced Catholicism and embraced Anglicanism, the colony reverted back to a proprietary form of government.

THE NEW ENGLAND COLONIES

After returning to England from Virgina in 1609, Capt. John Smith of the Virginia Company remained eager to explore and settle in America. He made contact with the Plymouth Company and sailed in 1614 to the area he named New England, carefully mapping the coast from Penobscot Bay to Cape Cod. On another exploratory voyage the following year, he was captured

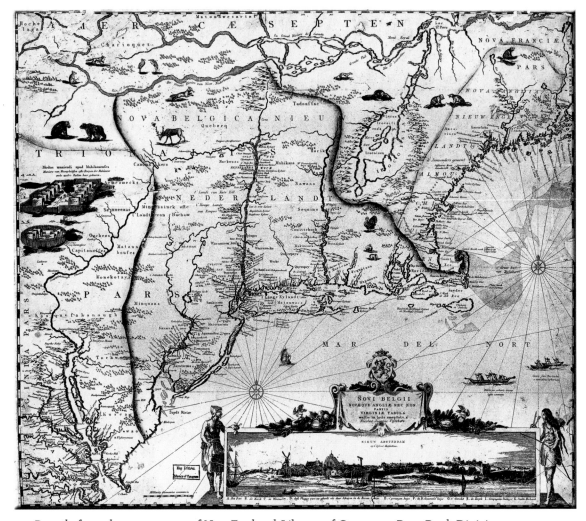

Detail of a 17th-century map of New England. Library of Congress, Rare Book Division

by pirates and returned to England after escaping three months later.

In 1617 he made one final colonizing attempt, but his vessels were unable to leave port for three months for lack of winds, and he never set sail. Although Smith never saw North America again, he advocated English settlement of New England for the rest of his life.

THE PILGRIMS

The first New England settlement was Plymouth in Massachusetts. Although lacking a charter, the founders of Plymouth were, like their counterparts in Virginia, dependent upon private investments from profit-minded backers to finance their colony. The nucleus of that settlement was drawn from an enclave of English émigrés in Leiden, Holland (now in the Netherlands). These religious Separatists believed that the true church was a voluntary company of the faithful under the "guidance" of a pastor and tended to be exceedingly individualistic in matters of church doctrine. Unlike the settlers of Massachusetts Bay, these Pilgrims chose to "separate" from the Church of England rather than to reform it from within.

In 1620, the first year of settlement, nearly half the Pilgrim settlers died of disease. From that time forward, however, and despite decreasing support from English investors, the health and the economic position of the colonists improved. The Pilgrims soon secured peace treaties with most of the Indians around them, enabling them to devote their time to building a strong, stable economic base rather than diverting their efforts toward costly and time-consuming problems of defending the colony from attack. Although none of their principal economic pursuits—farming, fishing, and trading—promised them lavish wealth,

The First Thanksgiving, reproduction of an oil painting by J.L.G. Ferris, early 20th century. Library of Congress, Washington, D.C. (neg. no. LC-USZC4-4961)

Document: William Bradford: Of Plymouth Plantation (1620–24)

William Bradford was the contemporary historian of a very small colony. About 100 persons reached Plymouth on the Mayflower *in December 1620. Thirty years later, at the completion of Governor Bradford's narrative, in 1650, the Plymouth colony still had fewer than 1,000 inhabitants. Book 1 of the narrative, which was completed about 1630, chronicles the events up to the landing at Plymouth. The remainder of the history was written between 1646 and 1651.*

The manuscript went at Bradford's death to his nephew, who loaned it to several of his contemporaries; it disappeared from the colonies during the Revolutionary War and finally came to light in 1855 in the library of the Bishop of London. Through the efforts of numerous diplomats and historians the original text was finally returned to America in 1897. It is now held by the State Library of Massachusetts in Boston.

They chose, or rather confirmed, Mr. John Carver (a man godly and well approved among them) their governor for that year. And after they had provided a place for their goods, or common store (which were long in unlading for want of boats, foulness of the winter weather, and sickness of diverse kinds), and begun some small cottages for their habitation, as time would admit, they met and consulted of laws and orders, both for their civil and military government as the necessity of their condition did require, still adding thereunto as urgent occasion in several times and as cases did require.

In these hard and difficult beginnings they found some discontents and murmurings arise among some, and mutinous speeches and carriages in other; but they were soon quelled and overcome by the wisdom, patience, and just and equal carriage of things by the governor and better part, which clave faithfully together in the main.

...But that which was most sad and lamentable was that in two or three months' time half of their company died, especially in January and February, being the depth of winter, and wanting houses and other comforts; being infected with the scurvy and other diseases which this long voyage and their inaccommodate condition had brought upon them. So as there died sometimes two or three of a day in the aforesaid time, that of one hundred and odd persons, scarce fifty remained. And of these, in the time of most distress, there were but six or seven sound persons who to their great commendations, be it spoken, spared no pains night or day, but with abundance of toil and hazard of their own health fetched them wood, made them fires, dressed them meat, made their beds, washed their loathsome clothes, clothed and and unclothed them. In a word, did all the homely and necessary offices for them which dainty and queasy stomachs cannot endure to hear named, and all this willingly and cheerfully, without any grudging in the least, showing herein their true love unto their friends and brethren; a rare example and worthy to be remembered...

the Pilgrims in America were, after only five years, self-sufficient.

Although the Pilgrims were always a minority in Plymouth, they nevertheless controlled the entire governmental structure of their colony during the first four decades of settlement. Before disembarking from the *Mayflower* in 1620, the Pilgrim founders, led by William Bradford, demanded that all the adult males aboard who were able to do so sign a compact promising obedience to the laws and ordinances drafted by the leaders of the enterprise. Although the Mayflower Compact has been interpreted as an important step in the evolution of democratic government in America, it is a fact that the compact represented a one-sided arrangement, with the settlers promising obedience and the Pilgrim founders promising very little. Although nearly all the male inhabitants were permitted to vote for deputies to a provincial assembly and for a governor, the colony, for at least the first 40 years of its existence, remained in the tight control of a few men. After 1660 the people of Plymouth gradually gained a greater voice in both their church and civic affairs, and by 1691, when Plymouth

Document: The Mayflower Compact (1620)

The voyagers on the Mayflower *were carried by wind and wave to a point—within the curve of the present Cape Cod—that was north of the Virginia Company's jurisdiction. Finding themselves thus outside the authority of their original patent and hoping to arrest mutinous talk among some of the passengers, a compact was drawn up and signed by 41 men aboard the ship, on Nov. 11, 1620.*

By the terms of this, the so-called Mayflower Compact, the Pilgrims agreed to govern themselves until they could arrange for a charter of their own. They were never able to arrange for such a charter, and the Compact remained in force until their colony at Plymouth was absorbed into that of Massachusetts Bay. (In fact, the Virginia Charter had been amended earlier in 1620, so as to allow for greater local autonomy. Had the Pilgrims landed at their original destination, they could still have formed their own government, as long as it was consonant with the laws of England.)

The original Compact has been lost, and historians are forced to rely for its wording in Mourt's Relation *(1622), which is the earliest source of the text reprinted here.*

This day, before we came to harbor, observing some not well affected to unity and concord, but gave some appearance of faction, it was thought good there should be an association and agreement that we should combine together in one body, and to submit to such government and governors as we should by common consent agree to make and choose, and set our hands to this that follows word for word.

In the name of God, Amen. We whose names are underwritten, the loyal subjects of our dread sovereign lord, King James, by the grace of God, of Great Britain, France, and Ireland, King, Defender of the Faith, etc.

Having undertaken for the glory of God, and advancement of the Christian faith and honor of our king and country, a voyage to plant the first colony in the northern parts of Virginia, do by these present, solemnly and mutually, in the presence of God and one of another, covenant and combine ourselves together into a civil body politic, for our better ordering and preservation and furtherance of the ends aforesaid; and by virtue hereof to enact, constitute, and frame such just and equal laws, ordinances, acts, constitutions, offices from time to time as shall be thought most meet and convenient for the general good of the colony; unto which we promise all due submission and obedience. In witness whereof we have hereunder subscribed our names, Cape Cod, 11th of November, in the year of the reign of our sovereign lord, King James, of England, France, and Ireland 18, and of Scotland 54. Anno Domini 1620.

The Journal of the Pilgrims at Plymouth in New England, in 1620, etc., etc., *George B. Cheever, ed., 2nd edition, New York, 1849, pp. 30–31.*

colony (also known as the Old Colony) was annexed to Massachusetts Bay, the Plymouth settlers had distinguished themselves by their quiet, orderly ways.

THE PURITANS

Like the Pilgrims, the Puritans of the Massachusetts Bay colony sailed to America principally to free themselves from religious restraints. Unlike the Pilgrims, the Puritans did not desire to "separate" themselves from the Church of England but, rather, hoped by their example to reform it. Nonetheless, one of the recurring problems facing the leaders of the Massachusetts Bay colony was the tendency of some, in their desire to free themselves from the alleged corruption of the Church of England, to espouse Separatist doctrine. When these tendencies or any other hint of deviation from orthodox Puritan doctrine developed, those holding them were either quickly corrected or expelled from the colony. The leaders of the Massachusetts Bay enterprise never intended their colony to be an outpost of toleration in the New World but, rather, a "Zion in the wilderness," a model of purity and orthodoxy, with all backsliders subject to immediate correction.

The civil government of the colony was guided by a similar authoritarian spirit. Men such as John Winthrop, the first governor of Massachusetts Bay, believed that it was the duty of the governors of society not to act as the direct representatives of their constituents but rather to decide, independently, what measures were in the best interests of the total society. The original charter of 1629 gave all power in the colony to a General Court composed of only a small number of shareholders in the company. On arriving in Massachusetts, many

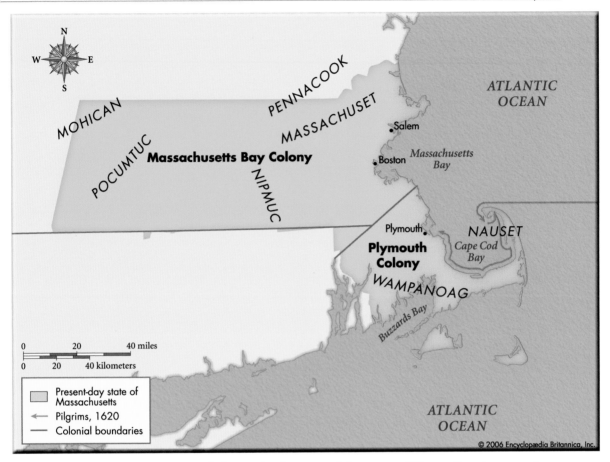

Map of Massachusetts Bay and Plymouth colonies, with locations of Native American peoples.

disfranchised settlers immediately pro-tested against this provision and caused the franchise to be widened to include all church members. These "freemen" were given the right to vote in the General Court once each year for a governor and a Council of Assistants. Although the char-ter of 1629 technically gave the General Court the power to decide on all matters affecting the colony, the members of the ruling elite initially refused to allow the freemen in the General Court to take part in the lawmaking process on the grounds that their numbers would render the court inefficient.

In 1634 the General Court adopted a new plan of representation whereby the freemen of each town would be permit-ted to select two or three delegates and assistants, elected separately but sitting together in the General Court, who would be responsible for all legislation. There was always tension existing between the smaller, more prestigious group of

Document: The Oath of a Freeman in Massachusetts (1634)

The Oath of a Freeman has dual historical significance. It was, in 1639, the first document printed on a press in America; and the second version of the oath, approved by the Massachusetts General Court May 14, 1634, contained a remarkably precise statement of the duties of a citizen toward his government. King Charles II objected to what he thought was an attitude of independence in the oath, which he attempted to subdue in 1665 by ordering that it be amended to include a pledge of "faith and true allegiance to our Sovereign Lord the King."

I...being by God's Providence an inhabitant and freeman within the jurisdiction of this commonwealth, do freely acknowledge myself to be subject to the government thereof; and therefore do swear by the great and dreadful name of the ever-living God that I will be true and faithful to the same, and will accordingly yield assistance and support thereunto with my person and estate, as in equity I am bound; and will also truly endeavor to maintain and preserve all the liberties and privileges thereof, submitting myself to the wholesome laws and orders made and established by the same. And further, that I will not plot or practise any evil against it, or consent to any that shall so do; but will timely discover and reveal the same to lawful authority now here established for the speedy preventing thereof.

Moreover, I do solemnly bind myself in the sight of God that, when I shall be called to give my voice touching any such matter of this state, in which freemen are to deal, I will give my vote and suffrage as I shall judge in my own conscience may best conduce and tend to the public weal of the body, without respect of persons or favor of any man. So help me God in the Lord Jesus Christ.

Tracts and Other Papers, Relating Principally to the Origin, Settlement, and Progress of the Colonies in North America, from the Discovery of the Country to the Year 1776, *Peter Force, ed., Washington, 1836–1846, IV: "New-Englands Jonas Cast up at London, etc., etc.," p. 18.*

assistants and the larger group of deputies. In 1644, as a result of this continuing tension, the two groups were officially lodged in separate houses of the General Court, with each house reserving a veto power over the other.

Despite the authoritarian tendencies of the Massachusetts Bay colony, a spirit of community developed there as perhaps in no other colony. The same spirit that caused the residents of Massachusetts to report on their neighbours for deviation from the true principles of Puritan morality also prompted them to be extraordinarily solicitous about their neighbours' needs. Although life in Massachusetts was made difficult for those who dissented from the prevailing orthodoxy, it was marked by a feeling of attachment and community for those who lived within the enforced consensus of the society.

DISSENSION

Many New Englanders, however, refused to live within the orthodoxy imposed by the ruling elite of Massachusetts. Both Connecticut and Rhode Island were founded as a by-product of their discontent.

The Rev. Thomas Hooker, who had arrived in Massachusetts Bay in 1633, soon found himself in opposition to the colony's restrictive policy regarding the admission of church members and to the oligarchic power of the leaders of the colony. Motivated both by a distaste for the religious and political structure of Massachusetts and a desire to open up new land, Hooker and his followers began moving into the Connecticut valley in 1635. By 1636 they had succeeded in founding three towns—Hartford, Windsor, and Wethersford. In 1638 the separate colony of New Haven was founded, and in 1662 Connecticut and Rhode Island merged under one charter.

Roger Williams, the man closely associated with the founding of Rhode Island, was banished from Massachusetts because of his unwillingness to conform to the orthodoxy established in that colony. Williams's views conflicted with those of the ruling hierarchy of Massachusetts in several important ways. His own strict criteria for determining who was regenerate, and therefore eligible for church membership, finally led him to deny any practical way to admit anyone into the church. Once he recognized that no church could ensure the purity of its congregation, he ceased using purity as a criterion and instead opened church membership to nearly everyone in the community. Moreover, Williams showed distinctly Separatist leanings, preaching that the Puritan church could not possibly achieve purity as long as it remained within the Church of England. Finally, and perhaps most serious, he openly disputed the right of the Massachusetts leaders to occupy

Document: Plan of Civil Government for Providence (1640)

Roger Williams, welcomed to Massachusetts in 1631 as a "godly minister," soon fell into disfavour for his criticisms of the civil governors in the Puritan colony. On Oct. 9, 1635, the Massachusetts General Court banished him from the colony for "propagating new and dangerous opinions." Williams and a small band of followers thus went, in 1636, to Narragansett Bay, where they founded the town of Providence. When they drew up the following plan of civil government in 1640, they determined the liberal character of the future Rhode Island colony in their pledge to "hold forth liberty of conscience" to all. This tolerant attitude caused other New England Puritans, who discouraged divergent religious beliefs within a single community, to look upon Providence as a veritable sink of iniquity.

We, Robert Coles, Chad Browne, William Harris, and John Warner, being freely chosen by the consent of our loving friends and neighbors, the inhabitants of this town of Providence, having many differences among us, they being freely willing and also bound themselves to stand to our arbitration in all differences among us, to rest contented in our determination being so betrusted, we have seriously and carefully endeavored to weigh and consider all those differences being desirous to bring to unity and peace, although our abilities are far short in the due examination of such weighty things; yet, so far as we conceive in laying all things together, we have gone the fairest and the equalest way to produce our peace.

I. *Agreed.* We have with one consent agreed that in the parting those particular properties which some of our friends and neighbors have in Pawtuxet, from the general common of our town of Providence to run upon a straight line from a fresh spring being in the gulley, at the head of that cove running by that point of land called Saxafras unto the town of Mashipawog to an oak tree standing near unto the cornfield, being at this time the nearest cornfield unto Pawtuxet, the oak tree having four marks with an axe, till some other landmark be set for a certain bound. Also, we agree that if any meadow ground lying and joining to that meadow that borders upon the river of Pawtuxet come within the foresaid line, which will not come within a straight line from Long Cove to the marked tree, then for that meadow to belong to Pawtuxet, and so beyond the town of Mashipawog from the oak tree between the two fresh rivers Pawtuxet and Wanasquatucket of an even distance...

land without first purchasing it from the Native Americans.

The unpopularity of Williams's views forced him to flee Massachusetts Bay for Providence in 1636. In 1639 William Coddington, another dissenter in Massachusetts, settled his congregation in Newport. Four years later Samuel Gorton, yet another minister banished from Massachusetts Bay because of his differences with the ruling oligarchy, settled in Shawomet (later renamed Warwick). In 1644 these three communities joined with a fourth in Portsmouth under one charter to become one colony called Providence Plantation in Narragansett Bay.

The early settlers of New Hampshire and Maine were also ruled by the government of Massachusetts Bay. New Hampshire was permanently separated from Massachusetts in 1692, although it was not until 1741 that it was given its own royal governor. Maine remained under the jurisdiction of Massachusetts until 1820.

THE MIDDLE COLONIES

New Netherland, founded in 1624 at Fort Orange (now Albany) by the Dutch West India Company, was but one element in a wider program of Dutch expansion in the first half of the 17th century. In 1664

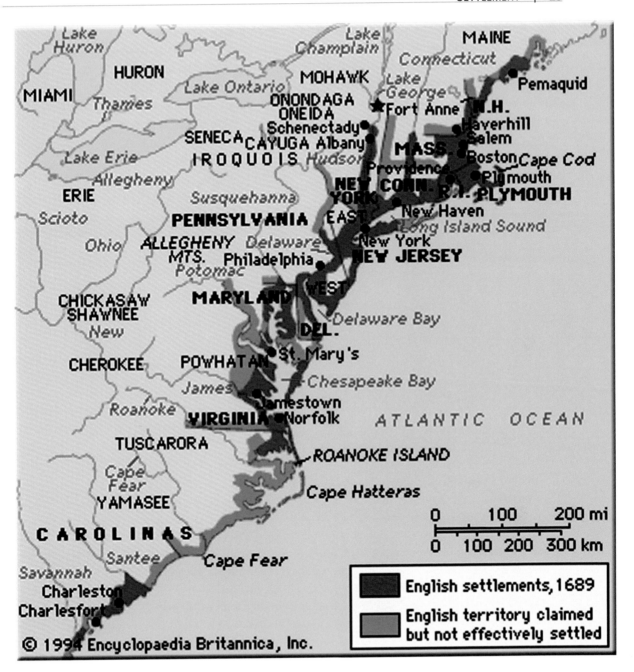

English colonies in 17th-century North America, with locations of Native American peoples..

the English captured the colony of New Netherland, renaming it New York after James, duke of York, brother of Charles II, and placing it under the proprietary control of the duke.

In return for an annual gift to the king of 40 beaver skins, the duke of York and his resident board of governors were given extraordinary discretion in the ruling of the colony. Although the grant to the duke of York made mention of a representative assembly, the duke was not legally obliged to summon it and in fact did not summon it until 1683. The duke's interest in the colony was chiefly economic, not political, but most of his efforts to derive economic gain from New York proved futile. Indians, foreign interlopers (the Dutch actually recaptured New York in 1673 and held it for more than a

Document: William Penn: The People Called Quakers (1696)

Primitive Christianity Revived was William Penn's attempt to show that the beliefs and practices of the Society of Friends were the same as those of the early Christian church, and were, in fact, the correct way to godliness. Penn emphasized the Quaker doctrine of the light of Christ in man, a "divine principle" that, even though it was not inherent in man's nature, was bestowed by God on all men. Accordingly, Quakers held in high regard humanitarian and equalitarian principles, because each individual carried within him a spark of Divine Spirit. The doctrine, which ascribed the Inner Light to all men, regardless of race or creed, marked the rise of a new religious liberalism and a spirit of toleration, especially in Pennsylvania.

That which the people called Quakers lay down as a main fundamental in religion is this, "That God, through Christ, has placed a principle in every man to inform him of his duty, and to enable him to do it; and that those that live up to this principle are the people of God; and those that live in disobedience to it are not God's people, whatever name they may bear or profession they may make of religion." This is their ancient, first, and standing testimony; with this they began, and this they bore, and do bear, to the world.

By this principle they understand something that is divine; and though in man, yet not of man, but of God; and that it came from Him, and leads to Him all those that will be led by it.

There are diverse ways of speaking they have been led to use, by which they declare and express what this principle is, about which I think fit to precaution the reader; viz., they call it "the light of Christ within man," or, "light within," which is their ancient, and most general and familiar phrase, also the manifestation or appearance of Christ; the witness of God, the seed of God; the seed of the kingdom; wisdom, the word in the heart; the grace that appears to all men; the spirit given to every man to profit with; the truth in the inward parts; the spiritual leaven that leavens the whole lump of man—which are many of them figurative expressions, but all of them such as the Holy Ghost had used, and which will be used in this treatise, as they are most frequently in the writings and ministry of this people...

year), and the success of the colonists in evading taxes made the proprietor's job a frustrating one.

In February 1685 the duke of York found himself not only proprietor of New York but also king of England, a fact that changed the status of New York from that of a proprietary to a royal colony. The process of royal consolidation was accelerated when in 1688 the colony, along with the New England and New Jersey colonies, was made part of the ill-fated Dominion of New England. In 1691 Jacob Leisler, a German merchant living on Long Island, led a successful revolt against the rule of the deputy governor, Francis Nicholson. The revolt, which was a product of dissatisfaction with a small aristocratic ruling elite and a more general dislike of the consolidated scheme of government of the Dominion of New England, served to hasten the demise of the dominion.

Pennsylvania, in part because of the liberal policies of its founder, William Penn, was destined to become the most diverse, dynamic, and prosperous of all the North American colonies. Penn himself was a liberal, but by no means radical, English Whig. His Quaker (Society of Friends) faith was marked not by the religious extremism of some Quaker leaders of the day but rather by an adherence to certain dominant tenets of the faith—liberty of conscience and pacifism—and by an attachment to some of the basic tenets of Whig doctrine. Penn sought to implement these ideals in his "holy experiment" in the New World.

Penn received his grant of land along the Delaware River in 1681 from Charles II as a reward for his father's service to the crown. The first "frame of government" proposed by Penn in 1682 provided for a council and an assembly, each to be elected by the freeholders of the colony. The council was to have the sole power of initiating legislation; the lower house could only approve or veto bills submitted by the council. After numerous objections about the "oligarchic" nature of this form of government, Penn issued a second frame of government in 1682 and then a third in 1696, but even these did not wholly satisfy the residents of the colony.

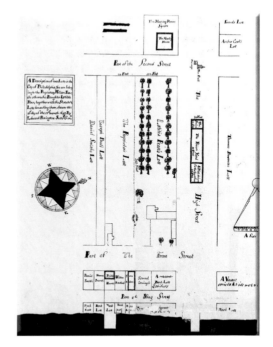

Diagram of lots of land in Philadelphia granted to William Penn and his daughter, 1698. Library of Congress, Washington, D.C.; map division

Title page from the German-language "An accurate description of the recently founded province of Pennsylvania" *written in 1700 by Francis Daniel Pastorius, who established the first German settlement in the colonies.* Library of Congress, Rare Book Division

Finally, in 1701, a Charter of Privileges, giving the lower house all legislative power and transforming the council into an appointive body with advisory functions only, was approved by the citizens. The Charter of Privileges, like the other three frames of government, continued to guarantee the principle of religious toleration to all Protestants.

Pennsylvania prospered from the outset. Although there was some jealousy between the original settlers (who had received the best land and important commercial privileges) and the later arrivals, economic opportunity in Pennsylvania was on the whole greater than in any other colony. Beginning in 1683 with the immigration of Germans into the Delaware valley and continuing with an enormous influx of Irish and Scotch-Irish in the 1720s and '30s, the population of Pennsylvania increased and diversified. The fertile soil of the countryside, in conjunction with a generous government land policy, kept immigration at high levels throughout the 18th century. Ultimately, however, the continuing influx of European settlers hungry for land spelled doom for the pacific Indian policy initially envisioned by Penn. "Economic opportunity" for European settlers often depended on the dislocation, and frequent extermination, of the American Indian residents who had initially occupied the land in Penn's colony.

New Jersey remained in the shadow of both New York and Pennsylvania throughout most of the colonial period. Part of the territory ceded to the duke of York by the English crown in 1664 lay in what would later become the colony of New Jersey. The duke of York in turn granted that portion of his lands to John Berkeley and George Carteret, two close friends and allies of the king. In 1665 Berkeley and Carteret established a proprietary government under their own direction. Constant clashes, however, developed between the New Jersey and the New York proprietors over the precise nature of the New Jersey grant. The legal status of New Jersey became even more tangled when Berkeley sold his half interest in the colony to two Quakers, who in turn placed the management of the colony in the hands of three trustees, one of whom was Penn. The area was then divided into East Jersey, controlled by Carteret, and West Jersey, controlled by Penn and the other Quaker trustees. In 1682 the Quakers bought East Jersey. A multiplicity of owners and an uncertainty of administration caused both colonists and colonizers to feel dissatisfied with the proprietary arrangement, and in 1702 the crown united the two Jerseys into a single royal province.

When the Quakers purchased East Jersey, they also acquired the tract of land that was to become Delaware, in order to protect their water route to Pennsylvania. That territory remained part of the Pennsylvania colony until 1704, when it was given an assembly of its own. It remained under the Pennsylvania governor, however, until the American Revolution.

Document: Anonymous: Opportunities for Settlers in Carolina (1666)

South Carolina was originally a proprietary colony—i.e., the rights of government were included in its grant—that was established on land given by Charles II in 1663 to eight of his friends. Some seven years passed before these proprietors could arrange for actual settlement, which began at Charles Town (Charleston) in 1670. In the interval, among other preparations, they arranged for and possibly wrote at least one pamphlet, of which a portion follows, setting forth the privileges they were prepared to grant to any settlers. A Brief Description of the Province of Carolina, on the Coasts of Floreda *was published in London in 1666.*

Carolina is a fair and spacious province on the continent of America.... The land is of diverse sorts as in all countries of the world. That which lies near the sea is sandy and barren, but bears many tall trees, which make good timber for several uses; and this sandy ground is by experienced men thought to be one cause of the healthfulness of the place. But up the river about twenty or thirty mile[s], where they have made a town, called Charles Town, there is plenty of as rich ground as any in the world.... The woods are stored with deer and wild turkeys, of a great magnitude, weighing many times above 50 lb. a piece, and of a more pleasant taste than in England, being in their proper climate; other sorts of beasts in the woods that are good for food, and also fowls, whose names are not known to them.

This is what they found naturally upon the place; but they have brought with them most sorts of seeds and roots of the Barbadoes which thrive [in] the most temperate clime...and they have potatoes, and the other roots and herbs of Barbadoes growing and thriving with them; as also from Virginia, Bermuda, and New England, what they could afford. They have indigo, tobacco, very good, and cotton wool; lime trees, orange, lemon, and other fruit trees they brought, thrive exceedingly. They have two crops of Indian corn in one year, and great increase every crop. Apples, pears, and other English fruit grow there out of the planted kernels....

THE CAROLINAS AND GEORGIA

The English crown had issued grants to the Carolina territory as early as 1629, but it was not until 1663 that a group of eight proprietors—most of them men of extraordinary wealth and power even by English standards—actually began colonizing the area. The proprietors hoped to grow silk in the warm climate of the Carolinas, but all efforts to produce that valuable commodity failed. Moreover, it proved difficult to attract settlers to the Carolinas; it was not until 1718, after a series of violent Indian wars had subsided, that the population began to increase substantially.

The pattern of settlement, once begun, followed two paths. North Carolina, which was largely cut off from the European and Caribbean trade by its unpromising coastline, developed into a colony of small to medium farms. South Carolina, with close ties to both the Caribbean and Europe, produced rice and, after 1742, indigo for a world market. The early settlers in both areas came primarily from the West Indian colonies. This pattern of migration was not, however, as distinctive in North Carolina, where many of the residents were part of the spillover from the natural expansion of Virginians southward.

The original framework of government for the Carolinas, the Fundamental Constitutions, drafted in 1669 by Anthony Ashley Cooper (Lord Shaftesbury) with the help of the philosopher John Locke, was largely ineffective because of its restrictive and feudal nature. The Fundamental Constitutions was abandoned in 1693 and replaced by a frame of government diminishing the powers of the proprietors and increasing the prerogatives of the provincial assembly. In 1729, primarily because of the proprietors' inability to meet the pressing problems of defense, the Carolinas were converted into the two separate royal colonies of North and South Carolina.

The proprietors of Georgia, led by James Oglethorpe, were wealthy philanthropic English gentlemen. It was Oglethorpe's plan to transport imprisoned debtors to Georgia, where they could rehabilitate themselves by profitable labour and make money for the proprietors in the process. Those who actually settled in Georgia—and by no means all of them were impoverished debtors—encountered a highly

Document: William Byrd: Surveying the Frontier (1728)

In his History of the Dividing Line, *William Byrd recorded the daily activities of a Virginia commission assigned to survey and relocate the boundary between Virginia and North Carolina. The 1728-29 survey was frequently hampered by quarrels with a North Carolina surveying party. Byrd placed the blame for these on the Carolinians, dubbing them "Knights of the Rum-Cask." The colourful background material in Byrd's* History, *which was not published until 1841, includes a sketch of the Virginia countryside and some caustic comments on the character of North Carolinians.*

March 9. The surveyors entered early upon their business this morning and ran the line through Mr. Eyland's plantation, as far as the banks of North River. They passed over it in the pirogue and landed in Gibbs's marsh, which was a mile in breadth and tolerably firm. They trudged through this marsh without much difficulty as far as the highland, which promised more fertility than any they had seen in these parts. But this firm land lasted not long before they came upon the dreadful pocoson [swamp] they had been threatened with. Nor did they find it one jot better than it had been painted to them. The beavers and otters had rendered it quite impassable for any creature but themselves.

Our poor fellows had much ado to drag their legs after them in this quagmire, but, disdaining to be balked, they could hardly be persuaded from pressing forward by the surveyors, who found it absolutely necessary to make a traverse in the deepest place to prevent their sticking fast in the mire and becoming a certain prey to the turkey buzzards.

This horrible day's work ended two miles to the northward of Mr. Merchant's plantation, divided from Northwest River by a narrow swamp, which is causewayed over. We took up our quarters in the open field not far from the house, correcting, by a fire as large as a Roman funeral pile, the aguish exhalations arising from the sunken grounds that surrounded us...

restrictive economic and social system. Oglethorpe and his partners limited the size of individual landholdings to 500 acres (about 200 hectares), prohibited slavery, forbade the drinking of rum, and instituted a system of inheritance that further restricted the accumulation of large estates. The regulations, though noble in intention, created considerable tension between some of the more enterprising settlers and the proprietors. Moreover, the economy did not live up to the expectations of the colony's promoters. The silk industry in Georgia, like that in the Carolinas, failed to produce even one profitable crop.

The settlers were also dissatisfied with the political structure of the colony; the proprietors, concerned primarily with keeping close control over their utopian experiment, failed to provide for local institutions of self-government. As protests against the proprietors' policies mounted, the crown in 1752 assumed control over the colony; subsequently, many of the restrictions that the settlers had complained about, notably those discouraging the institution of slavery, were lifted.

IMPERIAL ORGANIZATION

British policy toward the American colonies was inevitably affected by the domestic politics of England; since the politics of England in the 17th and 18th centuries were never wholly stable, it is not surprising that British colonial policy during those years never developed along clear and consistent lines. During the first half century of colonization, it was even more difficult for England to establish an intelligent colonial policy because of the very disorganization of the colonies themselves. It was nearly impossible for England to predict what role Virginia, Maryland, Massachusetts, Connecticut, and Rhode Island would play in the overall scheme of empire because of the diversity of the aims and governmental structures of those colonies. By 1660, however, England had taken the first steps in reorganizing her empire in a more profitable manner. The Navigation Act of 1660, a modification and amplification of a temporary series of acts passed in 1651, provided that goods bound to England or to English colonies, regardless of origin, had to be shipped only in English vessels; that three-fourths of the personnel of those ships had to be Englishmen; and that certain "enumerated articles," such as sugar, cotton, and tobacco, were to be shipped only to England, with trade in those items with other countries prohibited. This last provision hit Virginia and Maryland particularly hard; although those two colonies were awarded a monopoly over the English tobacco market at the same time that they were prohibited from marketing their tobacco elsewhere, there was no way that England alone could absorb their tobacco production.

The 1660 act proved inadequate to safeguard the entire British commercial empire, and in subsequent years other navigation acts were passed, strengthening the system. In 1663 Parliament passed an act requiring all vessels with European goods bound for the colonies to pass first through English ports to pay customs duties. In order to prevent merchants from shipping the enumerated articles from colony to colony in the coastal trade and then taking them to a foreign country, in 1673 Parliament required that merchants

post bond guaranteeing that those goods would be taken only to England. Finally, in 1696 Parliament established a Board of Trade to oversee Britain's commercial empire, instituted mechanisms to ensure that the colonial governors aided in the enforcement of trade regulations, and set up vice admiralty courts in America for the prosecution of those who violated the Navigation Acts. On the whole, this attempt at imperial consolidation—what some historians have called the process of Anglicization—was successful in bringing the economic activities of the colonies under closer crown control. While a significant amount of colonial trade continued to evade British regulation, it is nevertheless clear that the British were at least partially successful in imposing greater commercial and political order on the American colonies during the period from the late-17th to the mid-18th century.

In addition to the agencies of royal control in England, there were a number of royal officials in America responsible not only for aiding in the regulation of Britain's commercial empire but also for overseeing the internal affairs of the colonies. The weaknesses of royal authority in the politics of provincial America were striking, however. In some areas, particularly in the corporate colonies of New England during the 17th century and in the proprietary colonies throughout their entire existence, direct royal authority in the person of a governor responsible to the crown was nonexistent. The absence of a royal governor in those colonies had a particularly deleterious effect on the enforcement of trade regulations. In fact, the lack of royal control over the political and commercial activities of New England prompted the Board of Trade to overturn the Massachusetts Bay charter in 1684 and to consolidate Massachusetts, along with the other New England colonies and New York, into the Dominion of New England. After the colonists, aided by the turmoil of the Glorious Revolution of 1688 in England, succeeded in overthrowing the dominion scheme, the crown installed a royal governor in Massachusetts to protect its interests.

In those colonies with royal governors—the number of those colonies grew from one in 1650 to eight in 1760—the crown possessed a mechanism by which to ensure that royal policy was enforced. The Privy Council issued each royal governor in America a set of instructions carefully defining the limits of provincial authority. The royal governors were to have the power to decide when to call the provincial assemblies together, to prorogue, or dissolve, the assemblies, and to veto any legislation passed by those assemblies. The governor's power over other aspects of the political structure of the colony was just as great. In most royal colonies he was the one official primarily responsible for the composition of the upper houses of the colonial legislatures and for the appointment of important provincial officials, such as the treasurer, attorney general, and all colonial judges. Moreover, the governor had enormous patronage powers over the local agencies of government. The officials of the county court, who were the principal agents of local government, were appointed by the governor in most of the royal colonies. Thus, the governor had direct or indirect control over every agency of government in America.

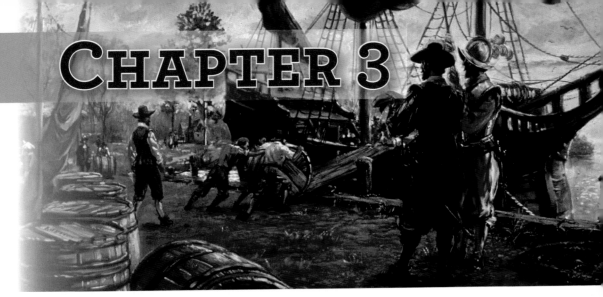

CHAPTER 3

THE GROWTH OF PROVINCIAL POWER

Royal governors found themselves frequently pulled in two directions. On one hand, they were responsible to the crown that had appointed them; on the other, they were constantly confronted by the needs and desires of the colonists. The distance separating England and America, the powerful pressures exerted on royal officials by Americans, and the inefficiency of large bureaucracy all served to weaken royal power and strengthen the hold of provincial leaders on the affairs of their respective colonies.

POLITICAL GROWTH

During the 18th century the colonial legislatures gained control over their own parliamentary prerogatives, achieved primary responsibility for legislation affecting taxation and defense, and ultimately took control over the salaries paid to royal officials. Provincial leaders also made significant inroads into the governor's patronage powers. Although theoretically the governor continued to control the appointments of local officials, in reality he most often automatically followed the recommendations of the provincial leaders in the localities in question. Similarly, the governor's councils, theoretically agents of royal authority, came to be dominated by prominent provincial leaders who tended to reflect the interests of the leadership of the lower house of assembly rather than those of the royal government in London.

Thus, by the mid-18th century most political power in America was concentrated in the hands of provincial rather than royal officials. These provincial leaders undoubtedly represented the interests of their constituents more faithfully than any royal official could, but it is clear that the politics of provincial America were hardly democratic by modern standards. In general, both social prestige and political power tended to be determined by economic standing, and the economic resources of colonial America, though not as unevenly distributed as in Europe, were nevertheless controlled by relatively few men.

In the Chesapeake Bay societies of Virginia and Maryland, and particularly in the regions east of the Blue Ridge mountains, a planter class came to dominate nearly every aspect of those colonies' economic life. These same planters, joined by a few prominent merchants and lawyers, dominated the two most important agencies of local government—the county courts and the provincial assemblies. This extraordinary concentration of power in the hands of a wealthy few occurred in spite of the fact that a large percentage of the free adult male population (some have estimated as high as 80 to 90 percent) was able to participate in the political process. The ordinary citizens of the Chesapeake society, and those of most colonies, nevertheless continued to defer to those whom they considered to be their "betters." Although the societal ethic that enabled power to be concentrated in the hands of a few was hardly a democratic one, there is little evidence, at least for Virginia and Maryland, that the people of those societies were dissatisfied with their rulers. In general, they believed that their local officials ruled responsively.

In the Carolinas a small group of planters monopolized much of the wealth. As in Virginia and Maryland, the planter class came to constitute a social elite. As a rule, the planter class of the Carolinas did not have the same long tradition of responsible government as did the ruling oligarchies of Virginia and Maryland, and, as a consequence, they tended to be absentee landlords and governors, often passing much of their time in Charleston, away from their plantations and their political responsibilities.

The western regions of both the Chesapeake and Carolina societies displayed distinctive characteristics of their own. Ruling traditions were fewer, accumulations of land and wealth less striking, and the social hierarchy less rigid in the west. In fact, in some western areas antagonism toward the restrictiveness of the east and toward eastern control of the political structure led to actual conflict. In both North and South

In 1682, William Penn, a British Quaker and proprietor of Pennsylvania, drew up a Frame of Government for the colony that would, he said, leave himself and his successors "no power of doing mischief, that the will of one man may not hinder the good of a whole country." Hulton Archive/Getty Images

Carolina armed risings of varying intensity erupted against the unresponsive nature of the eastern ruling elite. As the 18th century progressed, however, and as more men accumulated wealth and social prestige, the societies of the west came more closely to resemble those of the east.

New England society was more diverse and the political system less oligarchic than that of the South. In New England the mechanisms of town government served to broaden popular participation in government beyond the narrow base of the county courts.

The town meetings, which elected the members of the provincial assemblies, were open to nearly all free adult males. Despite this, a relatively small group of men dominated the provincial governments of New England. As in the South, men of high occupational status and social prestige were closely concentrated in leadership positions in their respective colonies; in New England, merchants, lawyers, and to a lesser extent clergymen made up the bulk of the social and political elite.

The social and political structure of the middle colonies was more diverse than that of any other region in America. New York, with its extensive system of manors and manor lords, often displayed genuinely feudal characteristics. The tenants on large manors often found it impossible to escape the influence of their manor lords. The administration of justice, the election of representatives, and the collection of taxes often took place on the manor itself. As a consequence, the large landowning families exercised an inordinate amount of economic and political power. The Great Rebellion of 1766, a short-lived outburst directed against the manor lords, was a symptom of the widespread discontent among the lower and middle classes.

By contrast, Pennsylvania's governmental system was more open and responsive than that of any other colony in America. A unicameral legislature, free from the restraints imposed by a powerful governor's council, allowed Pennsylvania to be relatively independent of the influence of both the crown and the proprietor. This fact, in combination with the tolerant and relatively egalitarian bent of the early Quaker settlers and the subsequent immigration of large numbers of Europeans, made the social and political structure of Pennsylvania more democratic but more faction-ridden than that of any other colony.

POPULATION GROWTH

The increasing political autonomy of the American colonies was a natural reflection of their increased stature in the overall scheme of the British Empire. In 1650 the population of the colonies had been about 52,000; in 1700 it was perhaps 250,000, and by 1760 it was approaching 1,700,000. Virginia had increased from about 54,000 in 1700 to approximately 340,000 in 1760. Pennsylvania had begun with about 500 settlers in 1681 and had attracted at least 250,000 people by 1760.

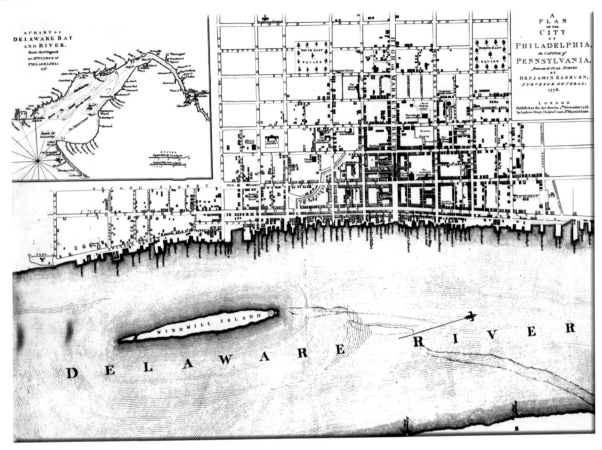

Map of Philadelphia, 1776. Library of Congress, Washington, D.C.

America's cities were beginning to grow as well. By 1765 Boston had reached 15,000; New York City, 16,000–17,000; and Philadelphia, the largest city in the colonies, 20,000.

Part of that population growth was the result of the involuntary immigration of African slaves. During the 17th century slaves remained a tiny minority of the population. By the mid-18th century, after Southern colonists discovered that the profits generated by their plantations could support the relatively large initial investments needed for slave labour, the volume of the slave trade increased markedly. In Virginia the slave population leaped from about 2,000 in 1670 to perhaps 23,000 in 1715 and reached 150,000 on the eve of the American Revolution. In South Carolina the jump was even more dramatic. In 1700 there were probably no more than 2,500 blacks in the population. By 1765 there were 80,000–90,000, with blacks outnumbering whites by about 2 to 1.

One of the principal attractions for the immigrants who moved to America voluntarily was the availability of inexpensive arable land. The westward migration to America's frontier—in the early 17th century all of America was a frontier, and by the 18th century the frontier ranged anywhere from 10 to 200 miles (15 to 320 km) from the coastline—was to become one of the distinctive elements in American history. English Puritans were the first to immigrate in large numbers to America, beginning in 1629 and continuing through 1640. Throughout the 17th century most of the immigrants were English, but by the second decade of the 18th century, a wave of Germans, principally from the Rhineland Palatinate, arrived in America. By 1770, between 225,000 and 250,000 Germans had immigrated to America, more than 70 percent of them settling in the middle colonies, where generous land policies and religious toleration made life more comfortable for them. The Scotch-Irish and Irish immigration, which began on a large scale after 1713 and continued past the American Revolution, was more evenly distributed. By 1750 both Scotch-Irish and Irish could be found in the western portions of nearly every colony.

In almost all the regions in which Europeans sought greater economic opportunity, however, that same quest for independence and self-sufficiency led to tragic conflict with Indians over the control of land. In nearly every instance the outcome was similar: the Europeans, failing to respect Indian claims either to land or to cultural autonomy, pushed the

Tobacco being transported by horse and boat. Library of Congress, Washington, D.C.

Indians of North America farther and farther to the periphery.

ECONOMIC GROWTH

Provincial America came to be less dependent upon subsistence agriculture and more on the cultivation and manufacture of products for the world market. Land, which initially served only individual needs, came to be the fundamental source of economic enterprise. The independent yeoman farmer continued to exist, particularly in New England and the middle colonies, but most settled land in North America by 1750 was devoted to the cultivation of a cash crop. New England turned its land over to the raising of meat products for export. The middle colonies were the principal producers of grains. By 1700 Philadelphia exported more than 350,000 bushels of wheat and more than 18,000 tons of flour annually.

The Southern colonies were, of course, even more closely tied to the cash crop system. South Carolina, aided by British incentives, turned to the production of rice and indigo. North Carolina, although less oriented toward the market economy than South Carolina, was nevertheless one of the principal suppliers of naval stores. Virginia and Maryland steadily increased their economic dependence on tobacco and on the London merchants who purchased that tobacco, and for the most part they ignored those who recommended that they diversify their economies by turning part of their land over to the cultivation of wheat. Their near-total dependence upon the world tobacco price would ultimately prove disastrous, but for most of the 18th century Virginia and Maryland soil remained productive enough to make a single-crop system reasonably profitable.

View of Boston in the 1760s. Library of Congress, Washington, D.C.

As America evolved from subsistence to commercial agriculture, an influential commercial class increased its power in nearly every colony. Boston was the centre of the merchant elite of New England, who not only dominated economic life but also wielded social and political power as well. Merchants such as James De Lancey and Philip Livingston in New York and Joseph Galloway, Robert Morris, and Thomas Wharton in Philadelphia exerted an influence far beyond the confines of their occupations. In Charleston the Pinckney, Rutledge, and Lowndes families controlled much of the trade that passed through that port. Even in Virginia, where a strong merchant class was nonexistent, those people with the most economic and political power were those commercial farmers who best combined the occupations of merchant and farmer.

It is clear that the commercial importance of the colonies was increasing. During the years 1700–10, approximately £265,000 sterling was exported annually to Great Britain from the colonies, with roughly the same amount being imported by the Americans from Great Britain. By the decade 1760–70, that figure had risen to more than £1,000,000 sterling of goods exported annually to Great Britain and £1,760,000 annually imported from Great Britain.

LAND, LABOUR, AND INDEPENDENCE

Although historian Frederick Jackson Turner's 1893 "frontier thesis"—that American democracy was the result of an abundance of free land—has long been seriously challenged and modified, it is clear that the plentifulness of virgin acres and the lack of workers to till them did cause a loosening of the constraints of authority in the colonial and early national periods. Once it became clear that the easiest path to success for Britain's New World "plantations" lay in raising export crops, there was a constant demand for agricultural labour, which in turn spurred practices that, with the notable exception of slavery, compromised a strictly hierarchical social order.

In all the colonies—whether governed directly by the king, proprietors, or chartered corporations—it was essential to attract settlers and what governors had most plentifully to offer was land. Sometimes large grants were made to entire religious communities numbering in the hundreds or more. Sometimes tracts were allotted to wealthy men on the "head rights" (literally "per capita") system of so many acres for each family member they brought over. Few Englishmen or Europeans had the means to buy farms outright, so the simple sale of homesteads by large-scale grantees was less common than renting.

But there was another well-traveled road to individual proprietorship that also provided a workforce, which was the system of contract labour known as indentured service. Under it, an impecunious new arrival would sign on with a landowner for a period of service—commonly seven years—binding him to

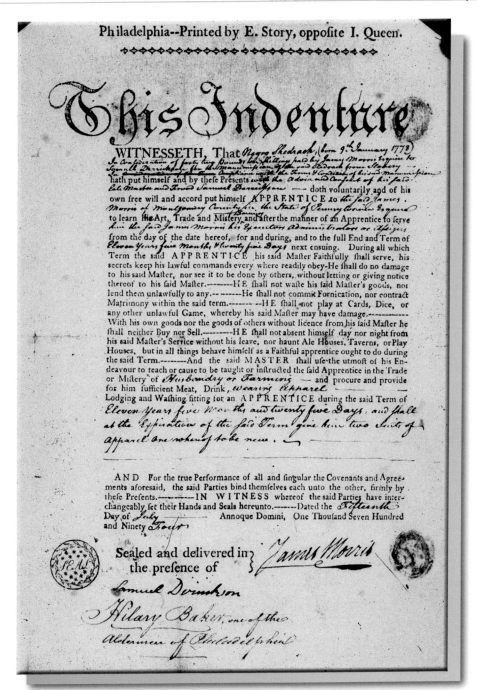

A certificate of indenture from 1794. Indentured servants worked in return for food and housing. At the end of the period of service, they frequently were granted their own plot of land. Kean Collection/Archive Photos/Getty Images

Document: Peter Fontaine: A Defense of Slavery in Virginia (1757)

By the middle of the 18th century, slaves had become an indispensable commodity on the tobacco, indigo, and rice plantations of Maryland, Virginia, and South Carolina. Many slaveholders deplored the ethics of the practice—but defended the use of slave labour as an economic necessity. One such apologist was the Rev. Peter Fontaine of Westover, Va., who discussed the subject in the following letter of March 30, 1757, to his brother Moses.

Now, to answer your first query—whether by our breach of treaties we have not justly exasperated the bordering nations of Indians against us, and drawn upon ourselves the barbarous usage we meet with from them and the French? To answer this fully would take up much time. I shall only hint at some things which we ought to have done, and which we did not do at our first settlement among them, and which we might have learned long since from the practice of our enemies the French.

I am persuaded we were not deficient in the observation of treaties, but, as we got the land by concession and not by conquest, we ought to have intermarried with them, which would have incorporated us with them effectually, and made of them staunch friends, and, which is of still more consequence, made many of them good Christians. But this our wise politicians at home put an effectual stop to at the beginning of our settlement here, for, when they heard that Rolfe had married Pocahontas, it was deliberated in Council whether he had not committed high treason by so doing, that is, marrying an Indian Princess. And had not some troubles intervened which put a stop to the inquiry, the poor man might have been hanged up for doing the most just, the most natural, the most generous and politic action that ever was done this side of the water. This put an effectual stop to all intermarriages afterward...

work in return for subsistence and sometimes for the repayment of his passage money to the ship captain who had taken him across the Atlantic. (Such immigrants were called "redemptioners.") At the end of this term, the indentured servant would, in many cases, be rewarded by the colony itself with "freedom dues," a title to 50 or more acres of land in a yet-unsettled area. This somewhat biblically inspired precapitalist system of transfer was not unlike apprenticeship, the economic and social tool that added to the supply of skilled labour. The apprentice system called for a prepubescent boy to be "bound out" to a craftsman who would take him into his own home and there teach him his art while serving as a surrogate parent. (Girls were perennially "apprenticed" to their mothers as homemakers.)

Both indentured servants and apprentices were subject to the discipline of the master, and their lot varied with his generosity or hard-fistedness. There must have been plenty of the latter type of master, as running away was common. The first Africans taken to Virginia, or at least some of them, appear to have worked as indentured servants. Not until the case of John Punch in the 1640s did it become legally established that black "servants" were to remain such for life. Having escaped, been caught, and brought to trial, Punch, an indentured servant of African descent, and two other indentured servants of European descent received very different sentences, with Punch's punishment being servitude for the "rest of his natural life" while that for the other two was merely an extension of their service.

The harshness of New England's climate and topography meant that for most of its people the road to economic independence lay in trade, seafaring, fishing, or craftsmanship. But the craving for an individually owned subsistence farm grew stronger as the first generations of religious settlers who had "planted" by congregation died off. In the process the communal holding of land by townships—with small allotted family garden plots and common grazing and orchard lands, much in the style of medieval communities—yielded gradually to the more conventional privately owned fenced farm. The invitation that available land offered—individual control of one's life—was irresistible. Property in land also conferred civic privileges, so

an unusually large number of male colonists were qualified for suffrage by the Revolution's eve, even though not all of them exercised the vote freely or without traditional deference to the elite.

Slavery was the backbone of large-scale cultivation of such crops as tobacco and hence took strongest root in the Southern colonies. But thousands of white freeholders of small acreages also lived in those colonies; moreover, slavery on a small scale (mainly in domestic service and unskilled labour) was implanted in the North. The line between a free and a slaveholding America had not yet been sharply drawn.

One truly destabilizing system of acquiring land was simply "squatting." On the western fringes of settlement, it was not possible for colonial administrators to use police powers to expel those who helped themselves to acres technically owned by proprietors in the seaboard counties. Far from seeing themselves as outlaws, the squatters believed that they were doing civilization's work in putting new land into production, and they saw themselves as the moral superiors of eastern "owners" for whom land was a mere speculative commodity that they did not, with great danger and hardship, cultivate themselves. Squatting became a regular feature of westward expansion throughout early U.S. history.

CHAPTER 4

CULTURAL AND RELIGIOUS DEVELOPMENT

A merica's intellectual attainments during the 17th and 18th centuries, while not inferior to those of the countries of Europe, were nevertheless of a decidedly different character. It was the techniques of applied science that most excited the minds of Americans, who, faced with the problem of subduing an often wild and unruly land, saw in science the best way to explain, and eventually to harness, those forces around them. Ultimately this scientific mode of thought might be applied to the problems of civil society as well, but for the most part the emphasis in colonial America remained on science and technology, not politics or metaphysics.

Typical of America's peculiar scientific genius was John Bartram of Pennsylvania, who collected and classified important botanical data from the New World. The American Philosophical Society, founded in 1744, is justly remembered as the focus of intellectual life in America. Men such as David Rittenhouse, an astronomer who built the first planetarium in America; Cadwallader Colden, the lieutenant governor of New York, whose accomplishments as a botanist and as an anthropologist probably outmatched his achievements as

The library of the American Philosophical Society in Philadelphia. Many early American intellectuals and innovators were members of the society, including cofounder Benjamin Franklin. Shutterstock.com

a politician; and Benjamin Rush, a pioneer in numerous areas of social reform as well as one of colonial America's foremost physicians, were among the many active members of the society.

At the centre of the society was one of its founders, Benjamin Franklin, who, in his experiments concerning the flow of electricity, proved to be one of the few American scientists to achieve a major theoretical breakthrough. Despite this fact, Franklin was more adept at the kinds of applied research that resulted in the manufacture of more efficient stoves and the development of the lightning rod.

LITERATURE, NEWSPAPERS, AND PERIODICALS

American cultural achievements in nonscientific fields were less impressive. American literature, at least in the traditional European forms, was nearly nonexistent. The most important American contribution to literature was neither in fiction nor in metaphysics but rather in such histories as Robert Beverley's *History and Present State of Virginia* (1705) or William Byrd's *History of the Dividing Line* (1728–29, but not published until 1841).

Document: Robert Beverley: Low Character of Immigrants to Virginia (1705)

Robert Beverley, considered one of the best early historians of Virginia, was asked by an English book dealer, in 1703, to appraise John Oldmixon's British Empire in America. So faulty did Beverley find the book that he set out to write his own interpretation of the Virginia he knew. The History and Present State of Virginia, published in 1705, is a sometimes humorous and often perceptive description of those "persons of low circumstances" who became the tobacco planters of early Virginia and who failed, in Beverley's opinion, to display a proper enterprising spirit.

I can easily imagine with Sir Josiah Child, that this, as well as all the rest of the plantations, was for the most part at first peopled by persons of low circumstances, and by such as were willing to seek their fortunes in a foreign country. Nor was it hardly possible it should be otherwise; for 'tis not likely that any man of a plentiful estate should voluntarily abandon a happy certainty to roam after imaginary advantages in a New World. Besides which uncertainty, he must have proposed to himself to encounter the infinite difficulties and dangers that attend a new settlement. These discouragements were sufficient to terrify any man that could live easy in England from going to provoke his fortune in a strange land.

Those that went over to that country first were chiefly single men, who had not the encumbrance of wives and children in England; and if they had, they did not expose them to the fatigue and hazard of so long a voyage, until they saw how it should fare with themselves. From hence it came to pass that, when they were settled there in a comfortable way of subsisting a family, they grew sensible of the misfortune of wanting wives, and such as had left wives in England sent for them; but the single men were put to their shifts. They excepted against the Indian women, on account of their being pagans, and for fear they should conspire with those of their own nation to destroy their husbands....

The most important cultural medium in America was not the book but the newspaper. The high cost of printing tended to eliminate all but the most vital news, and local gossip or extended speculative efforts were thus sacrificed so that more important material such as classified advertisements and reports of crop prices could be included, yet, Franklin, while wearing the hats of printer and journalist, managed to slip more than a little imaginative writing into the mix.

Next to newspapers, almanacs were the most popular literary form in America, Franklin's *Poor Richard's* being only the most famous among scores of similar projects. Not until 1741 and the first installment of Franklin's *General Magazine* did literary magazines begin to make their first appearance in America. Most of the 18th-century magazines, however, failed to attract subscribers, and nearly all of them collapsed after only a few years of operation.

Document: Benjamin Franklin: The Speech of Polly Baker (1747)

As the editor of a newspaper with space to fill, and as a printer with time occasionally on his hands, Benjamin Franklin wrote and published a variety of surreptitious pieces, pretending that their author was somebody else. The best known of these was a purported letter addressed to a friend, called Advice to a Young Man on the Choice of a Mistress *(1745). Only less famous, and widely circulated in its day, was* The Speech of Polly Baker *reprinted here, which appeared at Philadelphia in 1747 and also in the same year in a London magazine. There was no such trial as the Speech records, of course, nor any woman named Polly Baker. In point of fact, there was no law against bastardy in Connecticut. While Franklin may have intended a commentary on human affairs, he would only admit, many years later, to having sought the amusement of his readers.*

"May it please the Honorable Bench to indulge me in a few words. I am a poor, unhappy woman, who have no money to fee lawyers to plead for me, being hard put to it to get a tolerable living. I shall not trouble Your Honors with long speeches; nor have I the presumption to expect that you may, by any means, be prevailed on to deviate in your sentence from the law in my favor. All I humbly hope is that Your Honors would charitably move the governor's goodness in my behalf, that my fine may be remitted.

"This is the fifth time, gentlemen, that I have been dragged before your Court on the same account; twice I have paid heavy fines, and twice have been brought to public punishment for want of money to pay these fines. This may have been agreeable to the laws, and I don't dispute it; but since laws are sometimes unreasonable in themselves, and therefore repealed, and others bear too hard on the subject in particular instances, and therefore there is left a power somewhere to dispense with the execution of them, I take the liberty to say that I think this law, by which I am punished, is both unreasonable in itself, and particularly severe with regard to me, who have always lived an inoffensive life in the neighborhood where I was born, and defy my enemies (if I have any) to say I ever wronged any man, woman, or child... "

If Americans in the colonial period did not excel in achieving a high level of traditional cultural attainment, they did manage at least to disseminate what culture they had in a manner slightly more equitable than that of most countries of the world. Newspapers and almanacs, though hardly on the same intellectual level as the *Encyclopédie* produced by the European philosophes, probably had a wider audience than any European cultural medium.

VISUAL AND PERFORMING ARTS

The visual and performing arts, though flourishing somewhat more than literature, were nevertheless slow to achieve real distinction in America. The colonies

General Johnson Saving a Wounded French Officer by Benjamin West. In addition to providing a record of pre-Colonial America, West's paintings represent the height of New World achievement in the visual arts. Paul J. Richards/AFP/Getty Images

did produce one good historical painter in Benjamin West and two excellent portrait painters in John Copley and Gilbert Stuart, but it is not without significance that all three men passed much of their lives in London, where they received more attention and higher fees.

The Southern colonies, particularly Charleston, seemed to be more interested in providing good theatre for their residents than did other regions, but in no colony did the theatre approach the excellence of that of Europe. In New England, Puritan influence was an obstacle to the performance of plays, and even in cosmopolitan Philadelphia the Quakers for a long time discouraged the development of the dramatic arts.

EDUCATION

The New England colonies, although they did not always manage to keep pace with population growth, pioneered in the field of public education. Outside New England, education remained the preserve of those who could afford to send their children to private schools, although the existence of privately supported but tuition-free charity schools and of relatively inexpensive "academies" made it possible for the children of the American middle class to receive at least some education.

The principal institutions of higher learning—Harvard (1636), William and Mary (1693), Yale (1701), Princeton (1747), Pennsylvania (a college since 1755), King's

William and Mary College, engraved copperplate, c. 1740. Library of Congress, Washington, D.C.

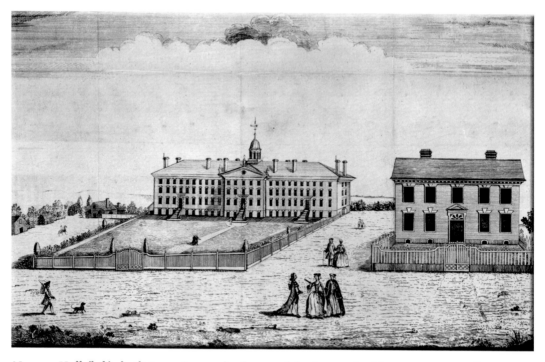

Nassau Hall (left), *built in 1756, was the first and the largest building at King's College (later Columbia University).* Library of Congress, Washington, D.C.

College (1754, now Columbia University), Rhode Island College (1764, now Brown University), Queen's College (1766, now Rutgers University), and Dartmouth (1769)—served the upper class almost exclusively; and most of them had a close relationship with a particular religious point of view (e.g., Harvard was a training ground for Congregational ministers, and Princeton was closely associated with Presbyterianism).

FROM A CITY ON A HILL TO THE GREAT AWAKENING

The part played by religion in the shaping of the American mind, while sometimes overstated, remains crucial. Over the first century and a half of colonial life, the strong religious impulses present in the original settlements—particularly those in New England—were somewhat secularized and democratized but kept much of their original power.

When the Pilgrim Fathers signed the Mayflower Compact in 1620, resolving themselves into a "civil body politic," they were explicitly making religious fellowship the basis of a political community. But even from the start, there were nonmembers of the Leiden Separatist congregation on the passenger list—the "strangers" among the "saints"—and they sought steady expansion of their rights

Document: John Eliot: A College Proposed for Massachusetts Bay (1633)

The religious zeal of the Massachusetts Bay Puritans was matched by their concern for the education of their youth, and after arriving in the New World they very soon began to discuss plans for establishing a school of higher learning, where their sons might prepare for the ministry and other professions. One of the earliest recorded expressions of this concern is a letter written in 1633 by John Eliot to Sir Simonds D'Ewes, in England. In the letter, reprinted here, Eliot, known for his missionary work among Native American communities, made a plea for funds that, had they been forthcoming, might have secured for D'Ewes the honor that later fell to John Harvard, i.e., having America's first college named after him.

I earnestly desire that God will move your heart for the sake of the commonwealth, and also for the sake of learning (which I know you love and will be ready to further; indeed, we want a store of men to further that, for if we do not nourish learning, both church and commonwealth will sink). Because I am on this point, I beseech you to let me be bold enough to make one motion, for the furtherance of learning among us.

God has bestowed upon you a bountiful blessing, and if you should please to employ one mite of that great wealth which God has given, to erect a school of learning—a college—among us, you would be doing a glorious work, acceptable to God and man, and the commemoration of the first founder of the means of learning would perpetuate your name and honor among us.

Now, because my proposition may seem to require great costs, I will be bold to propose a way that will make it attainable with little.

First, there are no improved lands and revenues at present to maintain such a work. All the charge is the building of such a place as may be fit for such a purpose. And such learned men as are here and may come must, of their own proper charge, frequent those places at fit seasons, for the exercising of learning; and such young men as may be trained must bear their own costs...

in Plymouth colony until its absorption into Massachusetts in 1691.

The Puritans were even more determined that their community be, as John Winthrop called it in his founding sermon, "A Model of Christian Charity," a "city on a hill," to which all humankind should look for an example of heaven on earth. This theme, in various guises, resounds in every corner of American history. The traditional image of Massachusetts Puritanism is one of repressive authority, but what is overlooked is the consensus among Winthrop and his followers that they *should* be bound together by love and shared faith, an expectation that left them "free" to do voluntarily what they all agreed was right. It was a kind of elective theocracy for the insiders.

The theocratic model, however, did not apply to nonmembers of the church, to whom the franchise was not originally

Document: Peter Bulkeley: A City Set Upon a Hill (1651)

According to the so-called doctrine of the Gospel Covenant—which combined political and religious ideas and which was articulated by the Rev. Peter Bulkeley in a sermon of the same name—the New England colonists enjoyed a special covenant with God and were therefore called upon to form a political and religious community wholly dedicated to Him. Those Puritans who embraced Arminianism tended to interpret the doctrine as an attempt to reconcile the Calvinist principle of salvation by God's grace alone with the principle that a man's right actions could influence God's attitude toward him. Bulkeley, a preacher at and one of the founders of Concord, Mass., maintained the Calvinist principle of predestination but qualified it by a strong emphasis on right living which he implied, if he did not explicitly assert, might win God's favour. This departure from strict Calvinism paved the way for the more liberal religious ideas of the 18th and 19th centuries.

Consider a time of separation must come wherein the Lord Jesus will divide and separate the holy from the unholy, as a shepherd separates the sheep from the goats. It will be good to be found among the saints at that day, and to stand in the assembly of the righteous. Woe, then, unto all those that are secluded from them, to all those that must stand without and be among dogs and devils, having no fellowship with Christ nor with his saints. It is good, therefore, to be holy. It will be found so then; woe unto the profane and ungodly at that day.

And for ourselves here, the people of New England, we should in a special manner labor to shine forth in holiness above other people. We have that plenty and abundance of ordinances and means of grace, as few people enjoy the like; we are as a city set upon a hill, in the open view of all the earth, the eyes of the world are upon us, because we profess ourselves to be a people in covenant with God, and therefore not only the Lord our God, with whom we have made covenant, but heaven and earth, angels and men, that are witnesses of our profession, will cry shame upon us if we walk contrary to the covenant which we have professed and promised to walk in. If we open the mouths of men against our profession, by reason of the scandalousness of our lives, we (of all men) shall have the greater sin...

extended, and problems soon arose in maintaining membership. Only those who had undergone a personal experience of "conversion" reassuring them of their salvation could be full members of the church and baptize their children. As the first generation died off, however, many of those children could not themselves personally testify to such conversion and so bring their own offspring into the church. They were finally allowed to do so by the Half-Way Covenant of 1662 but did not enjoy all the rights of full membership. Such apparent theological hair-splitting illustrated the power of the colony's expanding and dispersing population. As congregations hived off to different towns and immigration continued to bring in worshippers of other faiths, the rigidity of Puritan doctrine was forced to bend somewhat before the wind.

Nevertheless, in the first few years of Massachusetts's history, Puritan disagreements over the proper interpretation of doctrine led to schisms, exilings, and the foundation of new colonies. Only in America could dissenters move into neighbouring "wilderness" and start anew, as they did in Rhode Island and Connecticut. So the American experience encouraged religious diversity from the start. Even the grim practice of punishing dissidents such as the Quakers (and "witches") fell into disuse by the end of the 17th century.

Toleration was a slow-growing plant, but circumstances sowed its seeds early in the colonial experience. Maryland's founders, the well-born Catholic Calvert family, extended liberty to their fellow parishioners and other non-Anglicans in the Toleration Act of 1649. Despite the fact that Anglicanism was later established in Maryland, it remained the first locus of American Catholicism, and the first "American" bishop named after the Revolution, John Carroll, was of English stock. Not until the 19th century would significant immigration from Germany, Ireland, Italy, and Poland provide U.S. Catholicism its own "melting pot." Pennsylvania was not merely a refuge for the oppressed community who shared William Penn's Quaker faith but

by design a model "commonwealth" of brotherly love in general. And Georgia was founded by idealistic and religious gentlemen to provide a second chance in the New World for debtors in a setting where both rum and slavery were banned, though neither prohibition lasted long.

American Protestantism was also diversified by immigration. The arrival of thousands of Germans early in the 18th century brought, especially to western Pennsylvania, islands of German pietism as practiced by Mennonites, Moravians, Schwenkfelders, and others.

Anabaptists, also freshly arrived from the German states, broadened the foundations of the Baptist church in the new land. French Huguenots fleeing fresh persecutions after 1687 (they had already begun arriving in North America in the 1650s) added a Gallic brand of Calvinism to the patchwork quilt of American faith. Jews arrived in what was then Dutch New Amsterdam in 1654 and were granted asylum by the Dutch West India Company, to the dismay of Gov. Peter Stuyvesant, who gloomily foresaw that it would be a precedent for liberality toward Quakers, Lutherans, and "Papists." By 1763, synagogues had been established in New York, Philadelphia, Newport (R.I.), Savannah (Ga.), and other seaport cities where small Jewish mercantile communities existed.

Religious life in the American colonies already had a distinctive stamp in the 1740s. Some of its original zeal had cooled as material prosperity increased and the hardships of the founding era faded in memory. But then came a shake-up.

George Whitfield preaching to the masses. Whitfield was an influential figure during the Great Awakening, a series of mass religious revivals that spread across the colonies in the 1730s and 40s. The Bridgeman Art Library/Getty Images

A series of religious revivals known collectively as the Great Awakening swept over the colonies in the 1730s and '40s. Its impact was first felt in the middle colonies, where Theodore J. Frelinghuysen, a minister of the Dutch Reformed Church, began preaching in the 1720s. In New England in the early 1730s, men such as Jonathan Edwards, perhaps the most learned theologian of the 18th century, were responsible for a reawakening of religious fervour. By the late 1740s the movement had extended into the Southern colonies, where itinerant preachers such as Samuel Davies and George Whitefield exerted considerable influence, particularly in the backcountry.

The Great Awakening represented a reaction against the increasing secularization of society and against the corporate and materialistic nature of the principal churches of American society. By making conversion the initial step on the road to salvation and by opening up the conversion experience to all who recognized their own sinfulness,

Document: Jonathan Edwards: On the Great Religious Revival (1743)

Between 1730 and 1745 a religious revival known as the Great Awakening swept over the American colonies from Maine to Georgia. Particularly in the backcountry—where hundreds of isolated communities had neither church nor minister, and where the social instinct was all but wholly frustrated—a passion developed for religious conversion. Meetings were held and sects were formed, while itinerant preachers gave fervent sermons on the certainty of sin and the hope of salvation. The revival movement, unlike the earlier doctrine of the Puritans, promised the grace of God to all who could experience a desire for it.

Details of the Great Awakening in Northampton, Mass., are given in the following letter of Dec. 12, 1743, addressed by Jonathan Edwards to the Rev. Thomas Prince in Boston. The Mr. Whitefield to whom Edwards refers was the Rev. George Whitefield, the English evangelist who toured the American colonies in 1740 preaching to huge revival meetings. Admirers claimed he could make his voice audible to as many as 25,000 persons. Edwards's letter, which was printed by Prince in The Christian History *of January 14, 21, and 28, 1744, gives some indication of the reasons why in the following year Edwards started to cast doubt on the conversions within his own congregation—an act that virtually destroyed his public career.*

Ever since the great work of God that was wrought here about nine years ago, there has been a great abiding alteration in this town in many respects. There has been vastly more religion kept up in the town, among all sorts of persons, in religious exercises and in common conversation than used to be before. There has remained a more general seriousness and decency in attending the public worship. There has been a very great alteration among the youth of the town with respect to reveling, frolicking, profane and unclean conversation, and lewd songs. Instances of fornication have been very rare. There has also been a great alteration among both old and young with respect to tavern haunting. I suppose the town has been in no measure so free of vice in these respects for any long time together for this sixty years as it has been this nine years past.

There has also been an evident alteration with respect to a charitable spirit to the poor (though I think with regard to this we in this town, as the land in general, come far short of Gospel rules). And though after that great work nine years ago there has been a very lamentable decay of religious affections and the engagedness of people's spirit in religion, yet many societies for prayer and social religion were all along kept up; and there were some few instances of awakening and deep concern about the things of another world, even in the most dead time.

In the year 1740, in the spring, before Mr. Whitefield came to this town, there was a visible alteration. There was more seriousness and religious conversation, especially among young people; those things that were of ill tendency among them were more forborne...

the ministers of the Great Awakening, some intentionally and others unwittingly, democratized Calvinist theology. The technique of many of the preachers of the Great Awakening was to inspire in their listeners a fear of the consequences of their sinful lives and a respect for the omnipotence of God. This sense of the ferocity of God was often tempered by the implied promise that a rejection of worldliness and a return to faith would result in a return to grace and an avoidance of the horrible punishments of an angry God.

There was a certain contradictory quality about these two strains of Great Awakening theology, however. Predestination, one of the principal tenets of the Calvinist theology of most of the ministers of the Great Awakening, was ultimately incompatible with the promise that man could, by a voluntary act of faith, achieve salvation by his own efforts. Furthermore, the call for a return to complete faith and the emphasis on the omnipotence of God was the very antithesis of Enlightenment thought, which called for a greater questioning of faith and a diminishing role for God in the daily affairs of man. On the other hand, Edwards, one of the principal figures of the Great Awakening in America, explicitly drew on the thought of men such as John Locke and Isaac Newton in an attempt to make religion rational. Perhaps most important, the evangelical styles of religious worship promoted by the Great Awakening helped make the religious doctrines of many of the insurgent church denominations—particularly those of the Baptists and the Methodists—more accessible to a wider cross section of the American population. This expansion in church membership extended to blacks as well as to those of European descent, and the ritual forms of Evangelical Protestantism possessed features that facilitated the syncretism of African and American forms of religious worship.

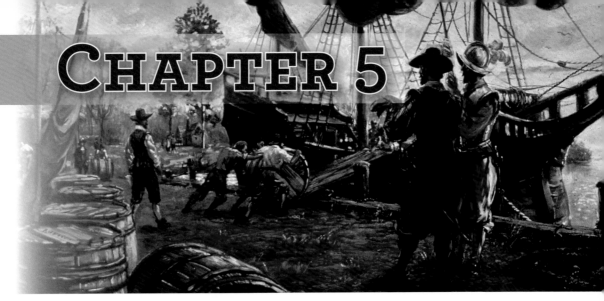

CHAPTER 5

COLONIAL AMERICA, ENGLAND, AND THE WIDER WORLD

The American colonies, though in many ways isolated from the countries of Europe, were nevertheless continually subject to diplomatic and military pressures from abroad. In particular, Spain and France were always nearby, waiting to exploit any signs of British weakness in America in order to increase their commercial and territorial designs on the North American mainland.

CONFLICT FOR TERRITORY

The Great War for the Empire—or the French and Indian War, as it is known to Americans—was but another round in a century of warfare between the major European powers. First in King William's War (1689–97), then in Queen Anne's War (1702–13), and later in King George's War (1744–48; the American phase of the War of the Austrian Succession), Englishmen and Frenchmen had vied for control over the Indians, for possession of the territory lying to the north of the North American colonies, for access to the trade in the Northwest, and for commercial superiority in the West Indies.

In most of these encounters, France had been aided by Spain. Because of its own holdings immediately south and west of the British colonies and in the Caribbean, Spain realized that it was in its own interest to join with the French in limiting British expansion.

THE GREAT WAR
FOR THE EMPIRE

The culmination of these struggles came in 1754 with the Great War for the Empire.

Whereas previous contests between Great Britain and France in North America had been mostly provincial affairs, with American colonists doing most of the fighting for the British, the Great War for the Empire saw sizable commitments of British troops to America. The strategy of the British under William Pitt was to allow their ally, Prussia, to carry the brunt of the fighting in Europe and thus free Britain to concentrate its troops in America.

Despite the fact that they were outnumbered 15 to 1 by the British colonial

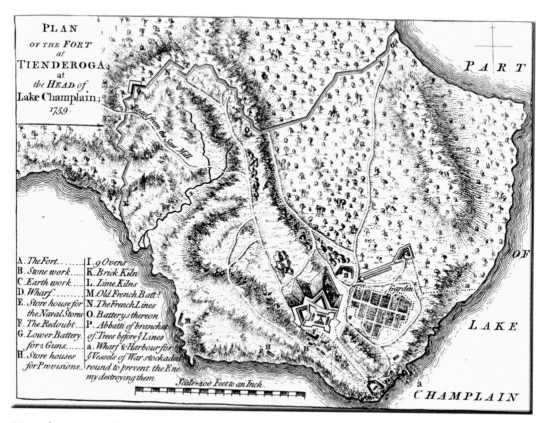

Map of Fort Ticonderoga, on Lake Champlain. Library of Congress, Washington, D.C.

An English engraving from 1775 celebrating the blockade of Louisbourg, Nova Scotia, during the French and Indian War. Library of Congress, Washington, D.C.

population in America, the French were nevertheless well equipped to hold their own. They had a larger military organization in America than did the English; their troops were better trained; and they were more successful than the British in forming military alliances with the Indians. The early engagements of the war went to the French; the surrender of George Washington to a superior French force at Fort Necessity, the annihilation of Gen. Edward Braddock at the Monongahela River, and French victories at Oswego and Fort William Henry all made it seem as if the war would be a short and unsuccessful one for the British. Even as these defeats took place, however, the British were able to increase their supplies of both men and matériel in America.

By 1758, with its strength finally up to a satisfactory level, Britain began to implement its larger strategy, which involved sending a combined land and sea force to gain control of the St. Lawrence and a large land force aimed at Fort Ticonderoga to eliminate French control of Lake Champlain. The first expedition against the French at Ticonderoga was a disaster, as Gen. James Abercrombie led

James Wolfe

The elder son of British Lieut. Gen. Edward Wolfe, James Wolfe was commissioned in the Royal Marines in 1741 but transferred almost immediately to the 12th Foot. Wolfe was on active service continuously until the end of the War of the Austrian Succession, fighting against the French at Dettingen (1743) and later at Falkirk and Culloden (1746) during the Jacobite rebellion. He was promoted to lieutenant colonel in 1750 and served as brigadier general under Maj. Gen. Jeffery Amherst in an expedition against the French at Cape Breton Island (1758). The capture of Louisbourg, a fortress on the island, was largely attributed to Wolfe's daring and determination.

Wolfe returned to England to restore his failing health, but there he received from William Pitt the rank of major general and command of the expedition to capture the city of

James Wolfe. Time & Life Pictures/Getty Images

Quebec. By late June 1759, Wolfe's entire convoy had passed up the St. Lawrence River and had reached the island of Orleans, which lay opposite Quebec along the river. The army of the French defender of Quebec, the marquis de Montcalm, was strongly entrenched on the high cliffs along the river frontage. Unable to lure Montcalm out from the safety of his defenses, Wolfe on July 31 ordered an assault on the Beauport shore east of the city, which proved to be a costly failure.

Ill with dysentery and suffering from rheumatism, Wolfe endured great pain and anxiety while the siege dragged on throughout August 1759. At the end of that month, he and his brigadiers agreed on a plan to land troops across the river a short distance upstream and to the west of Quebec. The resulting attack, which involved scaling the cliffs only one mile from the city, was carried out on September 12 and surprised the French on the level fields of the Plains of Abraham. On September 13, after a battle lasting less than an hour, the French fled. Wolfe, wounded twice early in the battle, died of a third wound, but not before he knew Quebec had fallen to his troops. Montcalm survived him by only a few hours. Quebec surrendered on September 18, and a year later in 1760 Amherst received the surrender of Montreal and the rest of Canada.

about 15,000 British and colonial troops in an attack against the French before his forces were adequately prepared. The British assault on Louisburg, the key to the St. Lawrence, was more successful. In July 1758 Lord Jeffery Amherst led a naval attack in which his troops landed on the shores from small boats, established beachheads, and then captured the fort at Louisburg.

In 1759, after several months of sporadic fighting, the forces of James Wolfe captured Quebec from the French army led by the marquis de Montcalm. This was probably the turning point of the war. By the fall of 1760, the British had taken Montreal, and Britain possessed practical control of all of the North American continent. It took another two years for Britain to defeat its rivals in other parts of the world, but the contest for control of North America had been settled.

AFTERMATH

In the Treaty of Paris of 1763, Great Britain took possession of all of Canada, East and West Florida, all territory east of the Mississippi in North America, and St. Vincent, Tobago, and Dominica in the Caribbean. At the time, the British victory seemed one of the greatest in its history. The British Empire in North America had been not only secured but also greatly expanded. But in winning the war Britain had dissolved the empire's most potent material adhesives. Conflicts arose as the needs and interests of the British Empire began to differ from those of the American colonies; and the colonies, now economically powerful, culturally distinct, and steadily becoming more independent politically, would ultimately rebel before submitting to the British plan of empire.

CHAPTER 6

THE NATIVE AMERICAN RESPONSE

The other major players in this struggle for control of North America were, of course, the American Indians. Modern historians no longer see the encounters between Native Americans and Europeans through the old lens in which "discoverers of a New World" find a "wilderness" inhabited by "savages." Instead they see a story of different cultures interacting, with the better-armed Europeans eventually subduing the local population, but not before each side had borrowed practices and techniques from the other and certainly not according to any uniform plan.

BRITISH RELATIONS WITH AMERICAN INDIANS

The English significantly differed from the Spanish and French colonizers in North America. Spain's widespread empire in the Southwest relied on scattered garrisons and missions to keep the Indians under control and "usefully"

A colour lithograph based on a painting done by American artist Frederic A. Chapman depicting Native Americans watching the 1609 voyage of Henry Hudson's ship. Library of Congress, Washington, D.C.

occupied. The French in Canada dealt with "their" Indians essentially as the gatherers of fur, who could therefore be left in de facto possession of vast forest tracts. English colonies, in what would eventually become their strength, came around to encouraging the immigration of an agricultural population that would require the exclusive use of large land areas to cultivate—which would have to be secured from native possessors.

English colonial officials began by making land purchases, but such transactions worked to the disadvantage of the Indians, to whom the very concept of group or individual "ownership" of natural resources was alien. After a "sale" was concluded with representatives of Indian peoples (who themselves were not always the "proprietors" of what they signed away), the Indians were surprised to learn that they had relinquished their hunting

Document: Samuel Sewall: On Accommodating the Indians (1700)

Samuel Sewall, jurist and Puritan leader, exhibited a rare but characteristic humanitarianism in his efforts to secure just treatment for the Native Americans residing in Massachusetts. In the following letter of May 3, 1700, Sewall expressed to Sir William Ashurst his concern with such practical problems as fixing fair boundaries for Indian lands, as well as a plan for recruiting missionaries from among those Native Americans converted to Christianity.

Last fall, I had notice of my being entrusted with a share in managing the Indian affairs, and presently upon it, the Commissioners were pleased to appoint me their secretary. As I account it an honor to be thus employed, so according to my mean ability, I shall endeavor faithfully to serve the Corporation and Commissioners, as I shall receive instructions from them.

I have met with an observation of some grave divines, that ordinarily when God intends good to a nation, He is pleased to make use of some of themselves to be instrumental in conveying of that good unto them. Now God has furnished several of the Indians with considerable abilities for the work of the ministry, and teaching school. And therefore I am apt to believe that if the Indians so qualified were more taken notice of in suitable rewards, it would conduce very much to the propagation of the Gospel among them. Besides the content they might have in a provision of necessary food and raiment, the respect and honor of it would quicken their industry and allure others to take pains in fitting themselves for a fruitful discharge of those offices.

One thing more I would crave leave to suggest. We have had a very long and grievous war with the Eastern Indians, and it is of great concernment to His Majesty's interests here that a peace be concluded with them upon firm and sure foundations; which in my poor opinion cannot well be while our articles of accord with them remain so very general as they do. I should think it requisite that convenient tracts of land should be set out to them; and that by plain and natural boundaries, as much as may be—as lakes, rivers, mountains, rocks—upon which for any Englishman to encroach should be accounted a crime...

and fishing rights, and settlers assumed an unqualified sovereignty that Native American culture did not recognize.

EUROPEAN-INDIAN ALLIANCES

In time, conflict was inevitable. In the early days of settlement, Indian-European cooperation could and did take place, as with, for example, the assistance rendered by Squanto to the settlers of Plymouth colony or the semidiplomatic marriage of Virginia's John Rolfe to Pocahontas, the daughter of Powhatan. The Native Americans taught the newcomers techniques of survival in their new environment and in turn were introduced

William Penn (dark coat) *purchases land from Delaware (Lenni Lanape) Indians that would become the Pennsylvania Colony. Penn's attempts to deal fairly with Native Americans were the exception rather than the rule among colonists.* Stock Montage/Archive Photos/Getty Images

to and quickly adopted metal utensils, European fabrics, and especially firearms. They were less adept in countering two European advantages—the possession of a common written language and a modern system of exchange—so most purchases of Indian lands by colonial officials often turned into thinly disguised landgrabs. William Penn and Roger Williams made particular efforts to deal fairly with the Native Americans, but they were rare exceptions.

The impact of Indian involvement in the affairs of the colonists was especially evident in the Franco-British struggle over Canada. For furs the French had depended on the Huron people settled around the Great Lakes, but the Iroquois Confederacy, based in western New York and southern Ontario, succeeded in crushing the Hurons and drove Huron allies such as the Susquehannocks and the Delawares southward into Pennsylvania. This action put the British in debt to the Iroquois because it diverted some of the fur trade from French Montreal and Quebec city to British Albany and New York City. European-Indian alliances also

A Native American trading furs for guns with French settlers in Canada. European alliances with specific tribes were often forged through strategic trade relationships. MPI/Archive Photos/ Getty Images

affected the way in which Choctaws, influenced by the French in Louisiana, battled with Spanish-supported Apalachees from Florida and with the Cherokees, who were armed by the British in Georgia.

AMERICAN INDIAN LEADERS

The French and Indian War not only strengthened the military experience and self-awareness of the colonists but also produced several Indian leaders, such as Red Jacket and Joseph Brant, who were competent in two or three languages and could negotiate deals between their own peoples and the European contestants. But the climactic Franco-British struggle was the beginning of disaster for the Indians. When the steady military success of the British culminated in the expulsion of France from Canada, the Indians no longer could play the diplomatic card of agreeing to support whichever king—the one in London or the one in Paris—would restrain westward settlement. Realizing this led some Indians to consider mounting a united resistance to further encroachments. This was the source of the rebellion led by the Ottawa chief Pontiac in 1763. However, as with later efforts at cooperative Indian challenges to European and, later, U.S. power, it simply was not enough.

Conclusion

By the middle of the 18th century, more and more colonial Americans had begun to view themselves as a breed apart. Those of English descent were still likely to think of themselves as English, and as such deserving of the rights and privileges guaranteed by English law. But they, and their fellow colonists with roots in Scotland, Ireland, Germany, the Low Countries, and elsewhere, saw themselves in another light, too. They were Virginians, New Yorkers, Pennsylvanians, and Georgians—not yet Americans with a shared identity and purpose, but a different sort of people who inhabited a New World full of possibilities and promise who would increasingly refuse to be bound by the expectations of the past.

Events would unfold to draw these disparate people ever closer together, although their union was no more inevitable than their independence. As the century progressed their fate became more, rather than less, precarious. Yet the country that arose in the decades to come—forged from sacrifice and courage, individual initiative and collective action—would grow to contribute some of the most dynamic chapters to human history.

CHRISTOPHER COLUMBUS: DISCOVERY OF THE NEW WORLD (1493)

Source: *Select Letters of Christopher Columbus: With Other Original Documents, Relating to his Four Voyages to the New World,*. R.H. Major, ed., London, 1847, pp. 1-17.

Knowing that it will afford you pleasure to learn that I have brought my undertaking to a successful termination, I have decided upon writing you this letter to acquaint you with all the events which have occurred in my voyage, and the discoveries which have resulted from it. Thirty-three days after my departure from [Gomera] I reached the Indian Sea, where I discovered many islands, thickly peopled, of which I took possession without resistance in the name of our most illustrious monarch, by public proclamation and with unfurled banners. To the first of these islands, which is called by the Indians Guanahani, I gave the name of the blessed Savior (San Salvador), relying upon whose protection I had reached this as well as the other islands; to each of these I also gave a name, ordering that one should be called Santa Maria de la Concepcion, another Fernandina, the third Isabella, the fourth Juana [Cuba], and so with all the rest....

As soon as we arrived at that, which as I have said was named Juana, I proceeded along its coast a short distance westward and found it to be so large and apparently without termination that I could not suppose it to be an island, but the continental province of Cathay. Seeing, however, no towns or populous places on the sea-coast, but only a few detached houses and cottages, with whose inhabitants I was unable to communicate because they fled as soon as they saw us, I went further on, thinking that in my progress I should certainly find some city or village.

At length, after proceeding a great way and finding that nothing new presented itself and that the line of coast was leading us northward (which I wished to avoid because it was winter, and it was my intention to move southward, and because, moreover, the winds were contrary), I resolved not to attempt any further progress but rather to turn back and retrace my course to a certain bay that I had observed, and from which I afterward dispatched two of our men to ascertain whether there were a king or any cities in that province. These men reconnoitered the country for three days and found a most numerous population and great numbers of houses, though small and built without any regard to order; with which information they returned to us. In the meantime I had learned from some Indians whom I had seized that that country was certainly an island, and therefore I sailed toward the east, coasting to the distance of 322 miles, which brought us to the extremity of it; from this point I saw lying eastward another island, 54 miles distant from Juana, to which I gave the name of Española [Hispaniola]. I went thither and steered my course eastward as I had done at Juana, even to the distance of 564 miles along the north coast....

In that island also, which I have before said we named Española, there are mountains of very great size and beauty, vast plains, groves, and very fruitful fields, admirably adapted for tillage, pasture, and habitation. The convenience and excellence of the harbors in this island and the abundance of the rivers, so indispensable to the health of man, surpass anything that would be believed by one who had not seen it. The trees, herbage, and fruits of Española are very different from those of Juana, and, moreover, it abounds in various kinds of spices, gold, and other metals.

The inhabitants of both sexes in this island, and in all the others which I have seen or of which I have received information, go always naked as they were born, with the exception of some of the women, who use the covering of a leaf or small bough or an apron of cotton which they prepare for that purpose. None of them, as I have already said, are possessed of any iron, neither have they weapons, being unacquainted with and

indeed incompetent to use them, not from any deformity of body (for they are well formed) but because they are timid and full of fear. They carry, however, in lieu of arms, canes dried in the sun, on the ends of which they fix heads of dried wood sharpened to a point, and even these they dare not use habitually; for it has often occurred when I have sent two or three of my men to any of the villages to speak with the natives, that they have come out in a disorderly troop and have fled in such haste at the approach of our men that the fathers forsook their children and the children their fathers. This timidity did not arise from any loss or injury that they had received from us; for, on the contrary, I gave to all I approached whatever articles I had about me, such as cloth and many other things, taking nothing of theirs in return; but they are naturally timid and fearful.

As soon, however, as they see that they are safe and have laid aside all fear, they are very simple and honest and exceedingly liberal with all they have; none of them refusing anything he may possess when he is asked for it, but, on the contrary, inviting us to ask them. They exhibit great love toward all others in preference to themselves. They also give objects of great value for trifles, and content themselves with very little or nothing in return. I, however, forbade that these trifles and articles of no value (such as pieces of dishes, plates, and glass, keys, and leather straps) should be given to them, although if they could obtain them, they imagined themselves to be possessed of the most beautiful trinkets in the world. It even happened that a sailor received for a leather strap as much gold as was worth three golden nobles, and for things of more trifling value offered by our men, especially newly coined blancas or any gold coins, the Indians would give whatever the seller required; as, for instance, an ounce and a half or two ounces of gold, or thirty or forty pounds of cotton, with which commodity they were already acquainted. Thus they bartered, like idiots, cotton and gold for fragments of bows, glasses, bottles, and jars, which I forbade as being unjust, and myself gave them many beautiful and acceptable articles which I had brought with me, taking nothing from them in return. I did this in order that I might the more easily conciliate them, that they might be led to become Christians and be inclined to entertain a regard for the King and Queen, our Princes, and all Spaniards, and that I might induce them to take an interest in seeking out and collecting and delivering to us such things as they possessed in abundance, but which we greatly needed. They practise no kind of idolatry, but have a firm belief that all strength and power, and indeed all good things, are in heaven, and that I had descended from thence with these ships and sailors, and under this impression was I received after they had thrown aside their fears. Nor are they slow or stupid, but of very clear understanding; and those men who have crossed to the neighboring islands give an admirable description of everything they observed;

but they never saw any people clothed nor any ships like ours.

On my arrival at that sea, I had taken some Indians by force from the first island that I came to, in order that they might learn our language and communicate to us what they knew respecting the country; which plan succeeded excellently and was a great advantage to us, for in a short time, either by gestures and signs or by words, we were enabled to understand each other. These men are still traveling with me, and although they have been with us now a long time, they continue to entertain the idea that I have descended from heaven; and on our arrival at any new place they published this, crying out immediately with a loud voice to the other Indians, "Come, come and look upon beings of a celestial race"; upon which both women and men, children and adults, young men and old, when they got rid of the fear they at first entertained, would come out in throngs, crowding the roads to see us, some bringing food, others drink, with astonishing affection and kindness.

Each of these islands has a great number of canoes, built of solid wood, narrow and not unlike our double-banked boats in length and shape, but swifter in their motion; they steer them only by the oar. These canoes are of various sizes, but the greater number are constructed with eighteen banks of oars, and with these they cross to the other islands, which are of countless number, to carry on traffic with the people. I saw some of these canoes that held as many as seventy-eight rowers. In all these islands there is no difference of physiognomy, of manners, or of language, but they all clearly understand each other, a circumstance very propitious for the realization of what I conceive to be the principal wish of our most serene King, namely, the conversion of these people to the holy faith of Christ, to which indeed, as far as I can judge, they are very favorable and well-disposed. I said before that I went 322 miles in a direct line from west to east, along the coast of the island of Juana, judging by which voyage, and the length of the passage, I can assert that it is larger than England and Scotland united; for independent of the said 322 miles there are in the western part of the island two provinces which I did not visit; one of these is called by the Indians Anam, and its inhabitants are born with tails....

But the extent of Española is greater than all Spain from Catalonia to Fontarabia, which is easily proved, because one of its four sides which I myself coasted in a direct line, from west to east, measures 540 miles. This island is to be regarded with special interest and not to be slighted; for although as I have said I took possession of all these islands in the name of our invincible King, and the government of them is unreservedly committed to His Said Majesty, yet there was one large town in Española of which especially I took possession, situated in a remarkably favorable spot and in every way convenient for the purposes of gain and commerce. To this town I gave the name of Navidad del Señor, and ordered a fortress to be built there, which must by this time be completed, in which I left as many men as I thought necessary, with all sorts of arms and enough provisions for more than a year. I also left them one caravel and skillful workmen, both in shipbuilding and other arts, and engaged the favor and friendship of the king of the island in their behalf, to a degree that would not be believed, for these people are so amiable and friendly that even the king took a pride in calling me his brother. But supposing their feelings should become changed and they should wish to injure those who have remained in the fortress, they could not do so, for they have no arms, they go naked, and are moreover too cowardly; so that those who hold the said fortress can easily keep the whole island in check, without any pressing danger to themselves, provided they do not transgress the directions and regulations which I have given them.

As far as I have learned, every man throughout these islands is united to but one wife, with the exception of the kings and princes, who are allowed to have twenty. The women seem to work more than the men. I could not clearly understand whether the people possess any private property, for I observed that one man had the charge of distributing various things to the rest, but especially meat and provisions and the like. I did not find, as some of us had expected, any cannibals among them, but, on the contrary, men of great deference and kindness. Neither are they black, like the Ethiopians; their hair is smooth and straight, for they do not dwell where the rays of the sun strike most vividly and the sun has intense power there, the distance from the equinoctial line being, it appears, but six-and-twenty degrees. On the tops of the mountains the cold is very great, but the effect of this upon the Indians is lessened by their being accustomed to the climate and by their frequently indulging in the use of very hot meats and drinks.

Thus, as I have already said, I saw no cannibals, nor did I hear of any, except in a certain island called Charis, which is the second from Española on the side toward India, where dwell a people who are considered by the neighboring islanders as most ferocious; and these feed upon human flesh. The same people have many kinds of canoes in which they cross to all the surrounding islands and rob and plunder wherever they can; they are not different from the other island-ers, except that they wear their hair long, like women, and make use of the bows and javelins of cane, with sharpened spearpoints fixed on the thickest end, which I have before described, and there-fore they are looked upon as ferocious and regarded by the other Indians with unbounded fear; but I think no more of them than of the rest. These are the men who form unions with certain women, who dwell alone in the island Matenin, which lies next to Española on the side toward India; these latter employ them-selves in no labor suitable to their own

sex, for they use bows and javelins as I have already described their paramours as doing, and for defensive armor have plates of brass, of which metal they pos-sess great abundance. They assure me that there is another island larger than Española, whose inhabitants have no hair, and which abounds in gold more than any of the rest. I bring with me indi-viduals of this island and of the others that I have seen, who are proofs of the facts which I state.

Finally, to compress into few words the entire summary of my voyage and speedy return and of the advantages derivable therefrom, I promise, that with a little assistance afforded me by our most invincible sovereigns, I will procure them as much gold as they need, as great a quantity of spices, of cotton, and of mas-tic (which is only found in Chios), and as many men for the service of the navy as Their Majesties may require. I promise also rhubarb and other sorts of drugs, which I am persuaded the men whom I have left in the aforesaid fortress have found already and will continue to find; for I myself have tarried no-where longer than I was compelled to do by the winds, except in the city of Navidad, while I pro-vided for the building of the fortress and took the necessary precautions for the perfect security of the men I left there.

Although all I have related may appear to be wonderful and unheard of, yet the results of my voyage would have been more astonishing if I had had at my disposal such ships as I required. But these great and marvelous results are not to be attributed to any merit of mine but to the holy Christian faith and to the piety and religion of our sovereigns; for that which the unaided intellect of man could not compass, the Spirit of God has granted to human exertions, for God is wont to hear the prayers of His servants who love His precepts even to the performance of apparent impossibilities. Thus it has happened to me in the present instance, who have accomplished a task to which the powers of mortal men had never hitherto attained; for if there have been those who have anywhere written or spoken of these islands, they have done so with doubts and conjectures, and no one has ever asserted that he has seen them, on which account their writings have been looked upon as little else than fables.

Therefore, let the King and Queen, our Princes, and their most happy kingdoms, and all the other provinces of Christendom render thanks to our Lord and Savior Jesus Christ, who has granted us so great a victory and such prosperity. Let processions be made and sacred feasts be held and the temples be adorned with festive boughs. Let Christ rejoice on earth, as He rejoices in heaven in the prospect of the salvation of the souls of so many nations hitherto lost. Let us also rejoice, as well on account of the exaltation of our faith as on account of the increase of our temporal prosperity, of which not only Spain but all Christendom will be partakers.

JOHN SMITH: STARVING TIME IN VIRGINIA (1607–14)

Source: *Works 1608–1631*, Edward Arber, ed., Birmingham, England, 1884, pp. 391–401, 497–516.

1607. Being thus left to our fortunes, it fortuned that within ten days scarce ten among us could either go or well stand, such extreme weakness and sickness oppressed us. And thereat none need marvel if they consider the cause and reason, which was this.

While the ships stayed, our allowance was somewhat bettered by a daily proportion of biscuits, which the sailors would pilfer to sell, give, or exchange with us for money, sassafras, furs, or love. But when they departed, there remained neither tavern, beer, house, nor place of relief, but the common kettle. Had we been as free from all sins as gluttony and drunkenness, we might have been canonized for saints; but our president [Wingfield] would never have been admitted for engrossing to his private [use] oatmeal, sack, aquavitae, beef, eggs, or what not, but the kettle; that indeed he allowed equally to be distributed, and that was half a pint of wheat, and as much barley boiled with water for a man a day, and this having fried some twenty-six weeks in the ship's hold, contained as many worms as grains; so that we might truly call it rather so much bran than corn, our drink was water, our lodgings castles in the air.

With this lodging and diet, our extreme toil in bearing and planting palisades so strained and bruised us, and our continual labor in the extremity of the heat had so weakened us, as were cause sufficient to have made us as miserable in our native country, or any other place in the world.

From May to September, those that escaped lived upon sturgeon, and sea crabs. Fifty in this time we buried, the rest seeing the president's projects to escape these miseries in our pinnace by flight (who all this time had neither felt want nor sickness) so moved our dead spirits, as we deposed him, and established Ratcliffe in his place (Gosnoll being dead), Kendall deposed. Smith newly recovered, Martin and Ratcliffe was by his care preserved and relieved, and the most of the soldiers recovered with the skillful diligence of Master Thomas Wolton, our chirurgeon [surgeon] general.

But now was all our provision spent, the sturgeon gone, all helps abandoned, each hour expecting the fury of the savages; when God, the Patron of all good endeavors in that desperate extremity so changed the hearts of the savages that they brought such plenty of their fruits and provision as no man wanted.

And now where some affirmed it was ill done of the Council to send forth men so badly provided, this incontradictable reason will show them plainly they are too ill advised to nourish such ill conceits. First, the fault of our going was our own; what could be thought fitting or necessary we had; but what we should find, or want, or where we should be, we were all ignorant, and supposing to make our passage in two months, with victual to live and the advantage of the spring to work. We were at sea five months, where we both spent our victual and lost the opportunity of the time and season to plant, by the unskillful presumption of our ignorant transporters, that understood not at all what they undertook. ...

And now, the winter approaching, the rivers became so covered with swans, geese, ducks, and cranes that we daily feasted with good bread, Virginia peas, pumpions [pumpkins], and putchamins [persimmons], fish, fowl, and diverse sorts of wild beasts as fat as we could eat them; so that none of our tuftaffety humorists desired to go for England.

But our comedies never endured long without a tragedy; some idle exceptions being muttered against Captain Smith for not discovering the head of the Chickahamania [Chickahominy] River, and taxed by the Council to be too slow in so worthy an attempt. The next voyage he proceeded so far that with much labor by cutting of trees asunder he made his passage; but when his barge could pass no farther, he left her in a broad bay out of danger of shot, commanding none should go ashore till his return. Himself, with two English and two savages, went up higher in a canoe; but he was not long absent but his men went ashore, whose want of government gave both occasion and opportunity to the savages to surprise one George Cassen, whom they slew, and much failed not to have cut off the boat and all the rest.

Smith, little dreaming of that accident, being got to the marshes at the river's head, twenty miles in the desert, had his two men slain (as is supposed) sleeping by the canoe, while himself, by fowling, sought them victual. Finding he was beset with 200 savages, two of them he slew still defending himself with the aid of a savage, his guide, whom he bound to his arm with his garters, and used him as a buckler, yet he was shot in his thigh a little, and had many arrows that stuck in his clothes; but no great hurt, till at last they took him prisoner. When this news came to Jamestown, much was their sorrow for his loss, few expecting what ensued.

Six or seven weeks those barbarians kept him prisoner, many strange triumphs and conjurations they made of him, yet he so demeaned himself among them as he not only diverted them from surprising the fort but procured his own liberty, and got himself and his company such estimation among them that those savages admired him more than their own *quiyouckosucks* [gods].

The manner how they used and delivered him is as follows:

The savages, having drawn from George Cassen whether Captain Smith was gone, prosecuting that opportunity, they followed him with 300 bowmen, conducted by the king of Pamaunkee, who, in divisions, searching the turnings of the river, found Robinson and Emry by the far side. Those they shot full of arrows and slew. Then finding the captain ... yet, dared they not come to him till, being near dead with cold, he threw away his arms. Then ... they drew him forth and led him to the fire, where his men were slain. Diligently, they chafed his benumbed limbs.

He demanding for their captain, they showed him Opechancanough, king of Pamaunkee, to whom he gave a round, ivory double compass dial. Much they marveled at the playing of the fly and needle, which they could see so plainly and yet not touch it because of the glass that covered them. But when he demonstrated by that globe-like jewel the roundness of the earth and skies, the sphere of the sun, moon, and stars, and how the sun did chase the night round about the world continually; the greatness of the land and sea, the diversity of nations, variety of complexions, and how we were to them antipodes, and many other suchlike matters, they all stood as amazed with admiration. Notwithstanding, within an hour after they tied him to a tree, and as many as could stand about him prepared to shoot him; but the king, holding up the compass in his hand, they all laid down their bows and arrows, and in a triumphant manner led him to [the town of] Orapaks, where he was after their manner kindly feasted and well used.

Their order in conducting him was thus: Drawing themselves all in file, the king in the middle had all their pieces and swords borne before him. Captain Smith was led after him by three great savages, holding him fast by each arm; and on each side, six went in file with their arrows nocked. But arriving at the town (which was but only thirty or forty hunting houses made of mats, which they remove as they please, as we our tents), all the women and children staring to behold him, the soldiers first, all in file and on each flank, officers ... to see them keep their orders. A good time they continued this exercise, and then cast themselves in a ring, dancing in such several postures, and singing and yelling out such hellish notes and screeches; being strangely painted, everyone his quiver of arrows, and at his back a club; on his arm a fox or an otter's skin ... their heads and shoulders painted red ... which scarlet-like color made an exceeding handsome show; his bow in his hand, and the skin of a bird with her wings abroad dried, tied on his. head, a piece of copper, a white shell, a long feather, with a small rattle growing at the tails of their snakes tied to it, or some suchlike toy.

All this while, Smith and the king stood in the middle, guarded, as before is said; and after three dances they all departed. Smith they conducted to a longhouse, where thirty or forty tall fellows did guard him; and ere long more bread and venison was brought him than would have served twenty men. I think his stomach at that time was not very good; what he left they put in baskets and tied over his head. About midnight they set the meat again before him, all this time not one of them would eat a bite with him, till the next morning they

brought him as much more; and then did they eat all the old, and reserved the new as they had done the other, which made him think they would fat him to eat him. Yet in this desperate estate to defend him from the cold, one ... brought him his gown, in requital of some beads and toys Smith had given him at his first arrival in Virginia.

Two days after, a man would have slain him (but that the guard prevented it) for the death of his son, to whom they conducted him to recover the poor man then breathing his last. Smith told them that at Jamestown he had a water would do it, if they would let him fetch it, but they would not permit that; but made all the preparations they could to assault Jamestown craving his advice; and for recompense he should have life, liberty, land, and women. In part of a tablebook he wrote his mind to them at the Fort, what was intended, how they should follow that direction to affright the messengers, and without fail send him such things as he wrote for and an inventory with them. The difficulty and danger, he told the savages, of the mines, great guns, and other engines exceedingly affrighted them, yet according to his request they went to Jamestown in as bitter weather as could be of frost and snow, and within three days returned with an answer.

But when they came to Jamestown, seeing men sally out as he had told them they would, they fled; yet in the night they came again to the same place where he had told them they should receive an answer, and such things as he had

promised them; which they found accordingly, and with which they returned with
no small expedition, to the wonder of
them all that heard it, that he could either
divine, or the paper could speak....

Not long after, early in the morning,
a great fire was made in a longhouse, and
a mat spread on the one side, as on the
other; on the one they caused him to sit,
and all the guard went out of the house,
and presently came skipping in a great
grim fellow, all painted over with coal,
mingled with oil, and many snakes' and
weasels' skins stuffed with moss, and all
their tails tied together, so as they met
on the crown of his head in a tassel; and
round about the tassel was as a coronet
of feathers, the skins hanging round
about his head, back, and shoulders, and
in a manner covered his face; with a hellish voice, and a rattle in his hand. With
most strange gestures and passions he
began his invocation, and environed the
fire with a circle of meal; which done,
three more suchlike devils came rush-
ing in with the like antic tricks, painted
half black, half red; but all their eyes were
painted white, and some red strokes like
Mutchato's along their cheeks. Round
about him those fiends danced a pretty
while, and then came in three more as
ugly as the rest, with red eyes and white
strokes over their black faces. At last they
all sat down right against him; three of
them on the one hand of the chief priest,
and three on the other.

Then all with their rattles began a
song, which ended, the chief priest laid
down five wheat corns. Then straining

his arms and hands with such violence
that he sweat, and his veins swelled, he
began a short oration; at the conclusion
they all gave a short groan, and then
laid down three grains more. After that,
began their song again, then another oration, ever laying down so many corns as
before, till they had twice encircled the
fire. That done, they took a bunch of little
sticks prepared for that purpose, continuing still their devotion, and at the end of
every song and oration, they laid down a
stick between the divisions of corn. Till
night, neither he nor they did either eat or
drink; and then they feasted merrily, with
the best provisions they could make.

Three days they used this ceremony;
the meaning whereof they told him was
to know if he intended them well or no.
The circle of meal signified their country,
the circles of corn, the bounds of the sea,
and the sticks, his country. They imagined the world to be flat and round, like a
trencher; and they in the middle.

After this they brought him a bag of
gun-powder, which they carefully preserved till the next spring, to plant as they
did their corn, because they would be
acquainted with the nature of that seed.

Opitchapam, the king's brother,
invited him to his house, where, with as
many platters of bread, fowl, and wild
beasts as did environ him, he bid him
welcome; but not any of them would eat
a bite with him, but put up remainder in
baskets.

At his return to Opechancanough's,
all the king's women and their children
flocked about him for their parts; as a

due by custom, to be merry with such fragments....

1608. At last they brought him to Meronocomoco, where was Powhatan, their emperor. Here more than 200 of those grim courtiers stood wondering at him, as he had been a monster; till Powhatan and his train had put themselves in their greatest braveries. Before a fire upon a seat like a bedstead, he sat covered with a great robe made of raccoon skins, and all the tails hanging by. On either hand did sit a young wench of sixteen or eighteen years, and along on each side the house, two rows of men, and behind them as many women, with all their heads and shoulders painted red, many of their heads bedecked with the white down of birds, but everyone with something, and a great chain of white beads about their necks. At his entrance before the king, all the people gave a great shout. The queen of Appamatuck was appointed to bring him water to wash his hands, and another brought him a bunch of feathers instead of a towel to dry them.

Having feasted him after their best barbarous manner they could, a long consultation was held, but the conclusion was: two great stones were brought before Powhatan; then as many as could laid hands on him, dragged him to them, and thereon laid his head, and being ready with their clubs to beat out his brains, Pocahontas, the king's dearest daughter, when no entreaty could prevail, got his head in her arms, and laid her own upon his to save his from death. Whereat the emperor was contented he should live to make him hatchets, and her bells, beads, and copper; for they thought him as well of all occupations as themselves. For the king himself will make his own robes, shoes, bows, arrows, pots; plant, hunt, or do anything so well as the rest....

Two days after, Powhatan having disguised himself in the most fearful manner he could, caused Captain Smith to be brought forth to a great house in the woods, and thereupon a mat by the fire, to be left alone. Not long after, from behind a mat that divided the house, was made the most doleful noise he ever heard; then Powhatan, more like a devil than a man, with some 200 more as black as himself, came unto him and told him now they were friends, and presently he should go to Jamestown to send him two great guns and a grindstone, for which he would give him the country of Capahowosick, and forever esteem him as his son Nantaquoud....

1609. The day before Captain Smith returned for England with the ships, Captain Davis arrived in a small pinnace, with some sixteen proper men more. To these were added a company from Jamestown, under the command of Captain John Sickelmore, alias Ratcliffe, to inhabit Point Comfort. Captain Martin and Captain West, having lost their boats and near half their men among the savages, were returned to James-town; for the savages no sooner understood Smith was gone but they all revolted, and did spoil and murder all they encountered.

Now we were all constrained to live only on that Smith had only for his own company, for the rest had consumed their proportions. And now they had twenty residents with all their appurtenances. Master Piercie, our new president, was so sick he could neither go nor stand. But ere all was consumed, Captain West and Captain Sickelmore, each with a small ship and thirty or forty men well appointed, sought abroad to trade. Sickelmore, upon the confidence of Powhatan, with about thirty others as careless as himself, were all slain; only Jeffrey Shortridge escaped; and Pocahontas, the king's daughter, saved a boy called Henry Spilman, that lived many years after, by her means, among the Patawomekes. Powhatan still, as he found means, cut off their boats, denied them trade; so that Captain West set sail for England.

Now we all found the loss of Captain Smith; yea, his greatest maligners could now curse his loss. As for corn provision and contribution from the savages, we had nothing but mortal wounds, with clubs and arrows. As for our hogs, hens, goats, sheep, horses, or what lived, our commanders, officers, and savages daily consumed them; some small proportions sometimes we tasted, till all was devoured. Then swords, arms, pieces, or anything we traded with the savages, whose cruel fingers were so oft imbrued in our blood, that what by their cruelty, our governor's indiscretion, and the loss of our ships, of 500 within six months after Captain Smith's departure there remained not past 60 men, women, and children — most miserable and poor creatures. And those were preserved for the most part by roots, herbs, acorns, walnuts, berries, now and then a little fish. They that had starch in these extremities made no small use of it; yea, even the very skins of our horses.

Nay, so great was our famine that a savage we slew and buried, the poorer sort took him up again and ate him; and so did diverse one another boiled and stewed with roots and herbs. And one among the rest did kill his wife, powdered [salted] her, and had eaten part of her before it was known; for which he was executed, as he well deserved. Now, whether she was better roasted, boiled, or carbonadoed [broiled], I know not; but of such a dish as powdered wife I never heard.

This was that time, which still to this day, we called the starving time. It were too vile to say, and scarce to be believed, what we endured; but the occasion was our own for want of providence, industry, and government, and not the barrenness and defect of the country, as is generally supposed. For till then in three years, for the numbers were landed us, we had never from England provision sufficient for six months, though it seemed by the bills of lading sufficient was sent us, such a glutton is the sea, and such good fellows the mariners. We as little tasted of the great proportion sent us as they of our want and miseries, yet, notwithstanding, they ever overswayed and ruled the business, though we endured all that is said, and chiefly lived on what this good country naturally afforded. Yet had we been even in Paradise itself with these governors, it would not have been much better with us; yet there was among us, who, had they had the government as Captain Smith appointed, but that they could not maintain it, would surely have kept us from those extremities of miseries. This in ten days more would have supplanted us all with death.

1610. But God, that would not this country should be unplanted, sent Sir Thomas Gates and Sir George Sommers with 150 people most happily preserved by the Bermudas to preserve us. Strange it is to say how miraculously they were preserved in a leaking ship....

1611. In the beginning of September 1611, he [Sir Thomas Dale] set sail, and arrived where he intended to build his new town. Within ten or twelve days he had environed it with a pale, and in honor of our noble Prince Henry called it Henrico. The next work he did was building at each corner of the town a high, commanding watchhouse, a church, and storehouses; which finished, he began to think upon convenient houses for himself and men, which, with all possible speed he could, he effected, to the great content of his company and all the colony.

This town is situated upon a neck of a plain rising land, three parts environed with the main river; the neck of land, well impaled, makes it like an isle. It has three streets of well-framed houses, a handsome church, and the foundation of a better laid (to be built of brick), besides storehouses, watchhouses, and suchlike. Upon the verge of the river there are five houses, wherein live the honester sort of people, as farmers in England, and they keep continual sentinel for the town's security. About two miles from the town, into the mainland, is another pale, nearly two miles in length, from river to river, guarded with several commanders, with a good quantity of corn-ground impaled, sufficiently secured to maintain more than I suppose will come this three years.

On the other side of the river, for the security of the town, is intended to be impaled for the security of our hogs, about two miles and a half, by the name of Hope in Faith, and Coxendale, secured by five of our manner of forts, which are but palisades, called Charity Fort, Mount Malado (a guesthouse [hospital] for sick people), a high seat and wholesome air, Elisabeth Fort, and Fort Patience. And here has Master Whitaker chosen his parsonage, impaled a fair-framed parsonage, and 100 acres called Rocke Hall, but these are not half finished.

About Christmas following, in this same year 1611, in regard of the injury done us by them of Appamatuck, Sir Thomas Dale, without the loss of any except some few savages, took it and their corn, being but five miles by land from Henrico; and considering how commodious it might be for us, resolved to possess and plant it, and at the instant called it the New Bermudas, whereunto he has laid out and annexed ... many miles of champion and woodland ground....

In the nether hundred he first began to plant; for there is the most corn-ground, and with a pale of two miles, cut over from river to river, whereby we have secured eight English miles in compass. Upon which circuit, within half a mile of each other, are many fair houses already built; besides particular men's houses near to the number of fifty. Rochdale, by a cross pale almost four miles long, is also planted with houses along the pale, in which hundred our hogs and cattle have [a] twenty-mile circuit to graze in securely. The building of the city is referred till our harvest be in, which he intends to make a retreat against any foreign enemy.

About fifty miles from these is Jamestown, upon a fertile peninsula, which, although formerly scandaled for an unhealthful air, we find it as healthful as any other part of the country. It has two rows of houses of framed timber, and some of them two stories and a garret higher; three large storehouses joined together in length; and he has newly strongly impaled the town. This isle, and much ground about it, is much inhabited. To Kecoughtan we accounted it forty miles, where they live well with half that allowance the rest have from the store, because of the extraordinary quantity of fish, fowl and deer....

1612. Since, there was a ship laden with provision and forty men; and another since then with the like number and provision, to stay twelve months in the country, with Captain Argall, which was sent not long after. After he had recreated and refreshed his company, he was sent to the River Patawomeke to trade for corn, the savages about us having small quarter, but friends and foes as they

found advantage and opportunity. But to conclude our peace, thus it happened. Captain Argall, having entered into a great acquaintance with Japazaws, an old friend of Captain Smith's, and so to all our nation, ever since he discovered the country, heard by him there was Pocahontas, whom Captain Smith's *Relations* entitles the nonpareil of Virginia. And though she had been many times a preserver of him and the whole colony, yet till this accident she was never seen at Jamestown since his departure.

1613. Being at Patawomeke, as it seems, thinking herself unknown, was easily by her friend Japazaws persuaded to go abroad with him and his wife to see the ship; for Captain Argall had promised him a copper kettle to bring her but to him, promising no way to hurt her but keep her till they could conclude a peace with her father. The savage, for this copper kettle, would have done anything, it seemed by the *Relations*. For though she had seen and been in many ships, yet he caused his wife to feign how desirous she was to see one, that he offered to beat her for her importunity, till she wept. But at last he told her if Pocahontas would go with her, he was content; and thus they betrayed the poor innocent Pocahontas aboard, where they were all kindly feasted in the cabin. Japazaws treading oft on the captain's foot to remember he had done his part.

The captain, when he saw his time, persuaded Pocahontas to the gunroom, feigning to have some conference with Japazaws, which was only that she should not perceive he was any way guilty of her captivity. So sending for her again, he told her before her friends she must go with him and compound peace between her country and us before she ever should see Powhatan. Whereat, [Japazaws] and his wife began to howl and cry as fast as Pocahontas; that upon the captain's fair persuasions, by degrees pacifying herself, and Japazaws and his wife with the kettle and other toys, went merrily on shore, and she to Jamestown. A messenger forthwith was sent to her father, that his daughter Pocahontas he loved so dearly, he must ransom with our men, swords, pieces, tools, etc., he treacherously had stolen.

This unwelcome news much troubled Powhatan, because he loved both his daughter and our commodities well, yet it was three months after ere he returned us any answer; then by the persuasion of the Council, he returned seven of our men, with each of them an unserviceable musket, and sent us word that when we would deliver his daughter, he would make us satisfaction for all injuries done us, and give 500 bushels of corn, and forever be friends with us. That he sent, we received in part of payment, and returned him this answer: That his daughter should be well used; but we could not believe the rest of our arms were either lost or stolen from him, and, therefore, till he sent them, we would keep his daughter.

This answer, it seemed, much displeased him, for we heard no more from him for a long time after; when with Captain Argall's ship, and some other vessels belonging to the colony, Sir Thomas Dale, with 150 men well appointed, went up into his own river, to his chief habitation, with his daughter. With many scornful bravados they affronted us, proudly demanding why we came thither. Our reply was we had brought his daughter, and to receive the ransom for her that was promised, or to have it perforce. They, nothing dismayed thereat, told us we were welcome if we came to fight, for they were provided for us; but advised us, if we loved our lives, to retire, else they would use us as they had done Captain Ratcliffe. We told them we would presently have a better answer; but we were no sooner within shot of the shore than they let fly their arrows among us in the ship.

Being thus justly provoked, we presently manned our boats, went on shore, burned all their houses, and spoiled all they had we could find; and so the next day proceeded higher up the river, where they demanded why we burned their houses. And we, why they shot at us. They replied it was some straggling savage, with many other excuses, they intended no hurt, but were our friends. We told them we came not to hurt them but visit them as friends also. Upon this we concluded a peace, and forthwith they dispatched messengers to Powhatan, whose answer, they told us, we must expect four-and-twenty hours ere the messengers could return. Then they told us our men had run away for fear we would hang them, yet Powhatan's men were run after them. As for our swords and pieces, they should be brought us the next day, which was only but to delay time, for the next day they came not.

Then we went higher, to a house of Powhatan's called Matchot, where we saw about 400 men well appointed. Here they dared us to come on shore, which we did. No show of fear they made at all, nor offered to resist our landing, but walking boldly up and down among us, demanded to confer with our captain, of his coming in that manner, and to have truce till they could but once more send to their king to know his pleasure, which if it were not agreeable to their expectation, then they would fight with us, and defend their own as they could. Which was but only to defer the time, to carry away their provision. Yet we promised them truce till the next day at noon, and then, if they would fight with us, they should know when we would begin by our drums and trumpets.

Upon this promise, two of Powhatan's sons came into us to see their sister; at whose sight, seeing her well, though they heard to the contrary, they much rejoiced, promising they would persuade her father to redeem her, and forever be friends with us. And upon this, the two brethren went aboard with us; and we sent Master John Rolfe and Master Sparkes to Powhatan to acquaint him with the business. Kindly they were entertained, but not admitted to the presence of Powhatan, but they spoke with Opechancanough his brother and successor. He promised to do the best he could to Powhatan, all might be well. So it being April, and time to prepare our ground and set our corn, we returned to Jamestown, promising the forbearance

of their performing their promise till the next harvest.

1614. Long before this, Master John Rolfe, an honest gentleman and of good behavior, had been in love with Pocahontas, and she with him; which thing, at that instant, I made known to Sir Thomas Dale by a letter from him, wherein he entreated his advice, and she acquainted her brother with it, which resolution Sir Thomas Dale well approved. The bruit of this marriage came soon to the knowledge of Powhatan, a thing acceptable to him, as appeared by his sudden consent, for within ten days he sent Opachisco, an old uncle of hers, and two of his sons to see the manner of the marriage, and to do in that behalf what they were requested, for the confirmation thereof, as his deputy; which was accordingly done about the first of April. And ever since we have had friendly trade and commerce, as well with Powhatan himself as all his subjects.

Besides this, by the means of Powhatan, we became in league with our next neighbors, the Chickahamanias [Chickahominies], a lusty and a daring people, free of themselves. These people, so soon as they heard of our peace with Powhatan, sent two messengers with presents to Sir Thomas Dale and offered them his service, excusing all former injuries. Hereafter they would ever be King James's subjects, and relinquish the name of Chickahamania, to be called Tassautessus, as they call us, and Sir Thomas Dale [to be] their governor, as the king's deputy. Only they desired to be governed by their own laws, which is eight of their elders as his substitutes. This offer he kindly accepted, and appointed the day he would come to visit them.

When the appointed day came, Sir Thomas Dale and Captain Argall, with fifty men well appointed, went to Chickahamania, where we found the people expecting our coming. They used us kindly, and the next morning sat in council to conclude their peace upon these conditions:

First, they should forever be called Englishmen, and be true subjects to King James and his deputies.

Second, neither to kill nor detain any of our men nor livestock but bring them home.

Third, to be always ready to furnish us with 300 men against the Spaniards or any.

Fourth, they shall not enter our towns, but send word they are new Englishmen.

Fifth, that every fighting man, at the beginning of harvest, shall bring to our store two bushels of corn, for tribute, for which they shall receive so many hatchets.

Last, the eight chief men should see all this performed, or receive the punishment themselves. For their diligence they should have a red coat, a copper chain, and King James's picture, and be accounted his nobleman.

All this they concluded with a general assent and a great shout to confirm it. Then one of the old men began an oration, bending his speech first to the old men, then to the young, and then to the women and children to make them understand how strictly they were to observe these conditions, and we would defend them from the fury of Powhatan, or any enemy whatsoever, and furnish them with copper, beads, and hatchets. But all this was rather for fear Powhatan and we, being so linked together, would bring them again to his subjection; the which to prevent, they did rather choose to be protected by us than tormented by him, whom they held a tyrant. And thus we returned again to Jamestown.

When our people were fed out of the common store and labored jointly together, glad was he who could slip from his labor, or slumber over his task he cared not how; nay, the most honest among them would hardly take so much true pains in a week as now for themselves they will do in a day. Neither cared they for the increase, presuming that howsoever the harvest prospered, the general store must maintain them, so that we reaped not so much corn from the labors of thirty as now three or four do provide for themselves. To prevent which, Sir Thomas Dale has allotted every man three acres of clear ground, in the nature of farms, except the Bermudas, who are exempted, but for one month's service in the year, which must neither be in seedtime nor harvest; for which doing, no other duty they pay to the store but two barrels and a half of corn.

From all those farmers (whereof the first was William Spence, an honest, valiant, and an industrious man, and has continued from 1607 to this present) from those is expected such a contribution to the store, as we shall neither want for ourselves, nor to entertain our supplies. For the rest, they are to work eleven months for the store, and have one month only allowed them to get provision to keep them for twelve, except two bushels of corn they have out of the store. If those can live so, why should any fear starving? And it were much better to deny them passage that would not, ere they come, be content to engage themselves to those conditions; for only from the slothful and idle drones, and none else, have sprung the manifold imputations Virginia innocently has undergone; and therefore I would deter such from coming here that cannot well brook labor, except they will undergo much punishment and penury, if they escape the scurvy. But for the industrious, there is reward sufficient, and if any think there is nothing but bread, I refer you to [Smith's] *Relations* that discovered the country first.

WILLIAM BRADFORD: *OF PLYMOUTH PLANTATION* (1620–24)

Source: Excerpt from *Of Plymouth Plantation 1620-1647*, Samuel Eliot Morison, ed., New York, 1963, pp. 23–334. Note: Subheads provided in Samuel Eliot Morison's carefully edited version of the manuscript.

They chose, or rather confirmed, Mr. John Carver (a man godly and well approved among them) their governor for that year. And after they had provided a place for their goods, or common store (which were long in unlading for want of boats, foulness of the winter weather, and sickness of diverse kinds), and begun some small cottages for their habitation, as time would admit, they met and consulted of laws and orders, both for their civil and military government as the necessity of their condition did require, still adding thereunto as urgent occasion in several times and as cases did require.

In these hard and difficult beginnings they found some discontents and murmurings arise among some, and mutinous speeches and carriages in other; but they were soon quelled and overcome by the wisdom, patience, and just and equal carriage of things by the governor and better part, which clave faithfully together in the main.

THE STARVING TIME

But that which was most sad and lamentable was that in two or three months' time half of their company died, especially in January and February, being the depth of winter, and wanting houses and other comforts; being infected with the scurvy and other diseases which this long voyage and their inaccommodate condition had brought upon them. So as there died sometimes two or three of a day in the aforesaid time, that of one hundred and odd persons, scarce fifty remained. And of these, in the time of most distress, there were but six or seven sound persons who to their great commendations, be it spoken, spared no pains night or day, but with abundance of toil and hazard of their own health fetched them wood, made them fires, dressed them meat, made their beds, washed their loathsome clothes, clothed and unclothed them. In a word, did all the homely and necessary offices for them which dainty and queasy stomachs cannot endure to hear named, and all this willingly and cheerfully, without any grudging in the least, showing herein their true love unto their friends and brethren; a rare example and worthy to be remembered. Two of these seven were Mr. William Brewster, their reverend elder, and Myles Standish, their captain and military commander, unto whom myself and many others were much beholden in our low and sick condition. And yet the Lord so upheld these persons as in this general calamity they were not at all infected either with sickness or lameness. And what I have said of these I may say of many others who died in this general visitation, and others yet living; that while they had health, yea, or any strength continuing, they were not wanting to any that had need of them. And I doubt not but their recompense is with the Lord....

INDIAN RELATIONS

All this while the Indians came skulking about them, and would sometimes show themselves aloof off, but when any approached near them, they would run away; and once they stole away their tools where they had been at work and were gone to dinner. But about the 16th of March, a certain Indian came boldly among them and spoke to them in broken English, which they could well understand but marveled at. At length they understood by discourse with him that he was not of these parts but belonged to the eastern parts where some English ships came to fish, with whom he was acquainted and could name sundry of them by their names, among whom he had got his language. He became profitable to them in acquainting them with many things concerning the state of the country in the east parts where he lived, which was after ward profitable unto them; as also of the people here, of their names, number and strength, of their situation and distance from this place, and who was chief among them. His name was Samoset. He told them also of another Indian whose name was Squanto, a native of this place, who had been in England and could speak better English than himself.

Being, after some time of entertainment and gifts dismissed, a while after he came again, and five more with him, and they brought again all the tools that were stolen away before, and made way for the coming of their great sachem, called Massasoit, who, about four or five days after, came with the chief, of his friends and other attendants, with the aforesaid Squanto; [and] with whom, after friendly entertainment and some gifts given him, they made a peace with him (which has now continued this twenty-four years) in these terms:

- That neither he nor any of his should injure or do hurt to any of their people.
- That if any of his did hurt to any of theirs, he should send the offender that they might punish him.
- That if anything were taken away from any of theirs, he should cause it to be restored; and they should do the like to his.
- If any did unjustly war against him, they would aid him; if any did war against them, he should aid them.
- He should send to his neighbors confederates to certify them of this that they might not wrong them, but might be like-wise comprised in the conditions of peace.
- That when their men came to them, they should leave their bows and arrows behind them.

After these things, he returned to his place called Sowams, some forty miles from this place, but Squanto continued with them and was their interpreter and was a special instrument sent of God for their good beyond their expectation. He directed them how to set their corn, where to take fish, and to procure other commodities, and was also their pilot to bring them to unknown places for their profit, and never left them till he died....

The spring now approaching, it pleased God the mortality began to cease among them, and the sick and lame recovered apace, which put, as it were, new life into them, though they had borne their sad affliction with much patience and contentedness as I think any people could do. But it was the Lord which upheld them and had beforehand prepared them, many having long borne the yoke, yea, from their youth. Many other smaller matters I omit, sundry of them having been already published in a journal made by one of the company, and some other passages of journeys and relations already published, to which I refer those that are willing to know them more particularly.

And being now come to the 25th of March, I shall begin the year 1621.

Mayflower Departs and Corn Planted

They now began to dispatch the ship away which brought them over, which lay till about this time, or the beginning of April. The reason on their part why she stayed so long was the necessity and danger that lay upon them; for it was well toward the end of December before she could land anything here, or they able to receive anything ashore.

Afterward, the 14th of January the house which they had made for a general rendezvous by casualty fell afire, and some were fain to retire aboard for shelter; then the sickness began to fall sore among them, and the weather so bad as they could not make much sooner any dispatch. Again, the governor and chief of them, seeing so many die and fall down sick daily, thought it no wisdom to send away the ship, their condition considered and the danger they stood in from the Indians, till they could procure some shelter; and therefore thought it better to draw some more charge upon themselves and friends than hazard all. The master and seamen likewise, though before they hasted the passengers ashore to be gone, now many of their men being dead, and of the ablest of them (as is before noted), and of the rest many lay sick and weak; the master dared not put to sea till he saw his men begin to recover, and the heart of winter over.

Afterward they (as many as were able) began to plant their corn, in which service Squanto stood them in great stead, showing them both the manner how to set it and after how to dress and tend it; also he told them, except they got fish and set with it in these old grounds, it would come to nothing. And he showed them that in the middle of April they should have store enough come up the brook by which they began to build, and taught them how to take it, and where to get other provisions necessary for them. All which they found true by trial and experience. Some English seed they sowed, as wheat and peas, but it came not to good, either by the badness of the seed or lateness of the season or both, or some other defect.

Bradford Succeeds Carver; Civil Marriage

In this month of April, while they were busy about their seed, their governor (Mr. John Carver) came out of the field very sick, it being a hot day. He complained greatly of his head and lay down, and within a few hours his senses failed, so as he never spoke more till he died, which was within a few days after; whose death was much lamented and caused great heaviness among them, as there was cause. He was buried in the best manner they could, with some volleys of shot by all that bore arms. And his wife, being a weak woman, died within five or six weeks after him.

Shortly after, William Bradford was chosen governor in his stead, and being not recovered of his illness, in which he had been near the point of death, Isaac Allerton was chosen to be an assistant unto him who, by renewed election every year, continued sundry years together. Which I here note once for all.

May 12 was the first marriage in this place which, according to the laudable custom of the Low Countries, in which they had lived, was thought most requisite to be performed by the magistrate, as being a civil thing, upon which many questions about inheritances do depend, with other things most proper to their cognizance and most consonant to the Scriptures (Ruth 4) and nowhere found in the Gospel to be laid on the ministers as a part of their office. "They decree or law about marriage was published by the States of the Low Countries Anno 1590. That those of any religion (after lawful and open publication) coming before the magistrates in the Town, or State house were to be orderly (by them) married one to another" (Petit's *History*, fol. 1029). And this practice has continued among not only them but has been followed by all the famous churches of Christ in these parts to this time—Anno 1646.

Indian Diplomacy

Having in some sort ordered their business at home, it was thought meet to send some abroad to see their new friend Massasoit, and to bestow upon him some gratuity to bind him the faster unto them; as also that hereby they might view the country and see in what manner he lived, what strength he had about him, and how the ways were to his place, if at any time they should have occasion. So the 2nd of July they sent Mr. Edward Winslow and Mr. Hopkins, with the aforesaid Squanto for their guide, who gave him a suit of clothes and a horseman's coat with some other small things, which were kindly accepted; but they found but short commons and came both weary and hungry home; for the Indians used then to have nothing so much corn as they have since the English have stored them with their hoes, and seen their industry in breaking up new grounds therewith.

They found his place to be forty miles from hence, the soil good and the people not many, being dead and abundantly wasted in the late great mortality which fell in all these parts about three years before the coming of the English, wherein thousands of them died. They not being able to bury one another, their skulls and bones were found in many places lying still above the ground where their houses and dwellings had been, a very sad spectacle to behold. But they brought word that the Narragansetts lived but on the other side of that great bay, and were a strong people and many in number, living compact together, and had not been at all touched with this wasting plague.

About the latter end of this month, one John Billington lost himself in the woods, and wandered up and down some five days, living on berries and what he could find. At length he [came] on an Indian plantation twenty miles south of this place, called Manomet. They conveyed him farther off, to Nauset among those people that had before set upon the English when they were coasting while the ship lay at the Cape, as is before noted. But the governor caused him to be inquired for among the Indians, and at length Massasoit sent word where he was, and the governor sent a shallop for him and had him delivered. Those people also came and made their peace; and they gave full satisfaction to those whose corn they had found and taken when they were at Cape Cod.

Thus their peace and acquaintance was pretty well established with the natives about them....

First Thanksgiving

They began now to gather in the small harvest they had, and to fit up their houses and dwellings against winter, being all well recovered in health and strength and had all things in good plenty. For as some were thus employed in affairs abroad, others were exercised in fishing, about cod and bass and other fish, of which they took good store, of which every family had their portion. All the summer there was no want; and now began to come in store of fowl, as winter approached, of which this place did abound when they came first (but afterward decreased by degrees). And besides waterfowl there was great store of wild turkeys, of which they took many, besides venison, etc. Besides they had about a peck of meal a week to a person, or now since harvest, Indian corn to that proportion. Which made many afterward write so largely of their plenty here to their friends in England, which were not feigned but true reports.

ARRIVAL OF THE *FORTUNE*

In November, about that time twelve-month that [they] themselves came, there came in a small ship [the *Fortune*] to them unexpected or looked for, in which came Mr. Cushman...and with him thirty-five persons to remain and live in the plantation; which did not a little rejoice them. And they, when they came ashore, and found all well and saw plenty of victuals in every house, were no less glad; for most of them were lusty young men, and many of them wild enough, who little considered whither or about what they went till they came into the harbor

at Cape Cod and there saw nothing but a naked and barren place. They then began to think what should become of them if the people here were dead or cut off by the Indians. They began to consult (upon some speeches that some of the seamen had cast out) to take the sails from the yard lest the ship should get away and leave them there. But the master, hearing of it, gave them good words and told them if anything but well should have befallen the people here, he hoped he had victuals enough to carry them to Virginia; and while he had a bit they should have their part, which gave them good satisfaction.

So they were all landed; but there was not so much as biscuit-cake or any other victuals for them, neither had they any bedding but some sorry things they had in their cabins; nor pot or pan to dress any meat in; nor overmany clothes, for many of them had brushed away their coats and cloaks at Plymouth as they came. But there was sent over some Birching Lane suits in the ship, out of which they were supplied. The plantation was glad of this addition of strength, but could have wished that many of them had been of better condition, and all of them better furnished with provisions. But that could not now be helped....

NARRAGANSETT CHALLENGE

Soon after this ship's departure, that great people of the Narragansetts, in a braving manner, sent a messenger unto them with a bundle of arrows tied about with a great snakeskin, which their interpreters told them was a threatening and a challenge. Upon which the governor, with the advice of others, sent them a round answer that if they had rather have war than peace, they might begin when they would; they had done them no wrong, neither did they fear them or should they find them unprovided; and by another messenger sent the snakeskin back with bullets in it. But they would not receive it, but sent it back again. But these things I do but mention because they are more at large already put forth in print by Mr. Winslow at the request of some friends. And it is like the reason was their own ambition who (since the death of so many of the Indians) thought to domineer and lord it over the rest, and conceived the English would be a bar in their way and saw that Massasoit took shelter already under their wings.

But this made them the more carefully to look to themselves, so as they agreed to enclose their dwellings with a good strong pale, and make flankers in convenient places with gates to shut, which were every night locked, and a watch kept; and when need required, there was also warding in the day time. And the company was, by the captain's and the governor's advice, divided into four squadrons, and everyone had their quarter appointed them unto which they were to repair upon any sudden alarm. And if there should be any cry of fire, a company were appointed for a guard, with muskets, while others quenched the same, to prevent Indian treachery. This

was accomplished very cheerfully, and the town impaled round by the beginning of March, in which every family had a pretty garden plot secured.

And herewith I shall end this year. only I shall remember one passage more, rather of mirth than of weight. On the day called Christmas Day, the governor called them out to work as was used. But the most of this new company excused themselves and said it went against their consciences to work on that day. So the governor told them that if they made it matter of conscience, he would spare them till they were better informed; so he led away the rest and left them. But when they came home at noon from their work, he found them in the street at play, openly; some pitching the bar, and some at stool-ball and suchlike sports. So he went to them and took away their implements and total them that was against his conscience that they should play and others work. If they made the keeping of it matter of devotion, let them keep their houses; but there should be no gaming or reveling in the streets. Since which time nothing has been attempted that way, at least openly....

The Fort Built; Visitors From Virginia Received

This summer they built a fort with good timber both strong and comely, which was of good defense, made with a flat roof and battlements, on which their ordnance were mounted, and where they kept constant watch, especially in time of danger.

It served them also for a meetinghouse and was fitted accordingly for that use. It was a great work for them in this weakness and time of wants, but the danger of the time required it; and both the continual rumors of the fears from the Indians here, especially the Narragansetts, and also the hearing of that great massacre in Virginia, made all hands willing to dispatch the same.

Now the welcome time of harvest approached, in which all had their hungry bellies filled. But it arose but to a little, in comparison of a full year's supply; partly because they were not yet well acquainted with the manner of Indian corn (and they had no other), also their many other employments; but chiefly their weakness for want of food, to tend it as they should have done. Also, much was stolen both by night and day before it became scarce eatable, and much more afterward. And though many were well whipped when they were taken for a few ears of corn, yet hunger made others, whom conscience did not restrain, to venture. So as it well appeared that famine must still ensue, the next year also if not some way prevented, or supply should fail, to which they dared not trust. Markets there were none to go to, but only the Indians, and they had no trading commodities

Behold, now, another Providence of God. A ship comes into the harbor, one Captain Jones being chief therein. They were set out by some merchants to discover all the harbors between this and Virginia and the shoals of Cape Cod, and to trade along the coast where they could.

This ship had store of English beads (which were then good trade) and some knives; but would sell none but at dear rates and also a good quantity together. Yet they were glad of the occasion and fain to buy at any rate; they were fain to give after the rate of cento per cento [100 percent], if not more; and yet pay away coat-beaver at 3s. per pound, which in a few years after yielded 20s. By this means they were fitted again to trade for beaver and other things, and intended to buy what corn they could....

After these things, in February a messenger came from John Sanders, who was left chief over Mr. Weston's men in the Bay of Massachusetts, who brought a letter showing the great wants they were fallen into; and he would have borrowed a hogshead of corn of the Indians but they would lend him none. He desired advice whether he might not take it from them by force to succor his men till he came from the eastward whither he was going. The governor and rest dissuaded him by all means from it, for it might so exasperate the Indians as might endanger their safety, and all of us might smart for it; for they had already heard how they had so wronged the Indians by stealing their corn, etc., as they were much incensed against them. Yea, so base were some of their own company as they went and told the Indians that their governor was purposed to come and take their corn by force. The which, with other things, made them enter into a conspiracy against the English, of which more in the next. Herewith I end this year.

Sad Straits of Weston's Men and the Great Indian Conspiracy

It may be thought strange that these people should fall to these extremities in so short a time, being left competently provided when the ship left them, and had an ambition by that moiety of corn that was got by trade, besides much they got of the Indians where they lived, by one means and other. It must needs be their great disorder, for they spent excessively while they had or could get it; and, it may be, wasted part away among the Indians; for he that was their chief was taxed by some among them for keeping Indian women, how truly I know not. And after they began to come into wants, many sold away their clothes and bed coverings; others (so base were they) became servants to the Indians, and would cut them wood and fetch them water for a capful of corn; others fell to plain stealing, both night and day, from the Indians, of which they grievously complained. In the end, they came to that misery that some starved and died with cold and hunger. One, in gathering shellfish, was so weak as he stuck fast in the mud and was found dead in the place. At last most of them left their dwellings and scattered up and down in the woods and by the water-sides, where they could find peanuts and clams, here six and there ten....

This was the end of these, that sometime boasted of their strength (being all able, lusty men) and what they would do and bring to pass in comparison of the people here, who had many women and children and weak ones among them; and said at their first arrival, when they saw the wants here, that they would take another course and not to fall into such a condition as this simple people were come to. But a man's way is not in his own power; God can make the weak to stand. Let him also that standeth take heed lest he fall....

End of the "Common Course and Condition"

All this while no supply was heard of, neither knew they when they might expect any. So they began to think how they might raise as much corn as they could and obtain a better crop than they had done, that they might not still thus languish in misery. At length, after much debate of things, the governor (with the advice of the chief among them) gave way that they should set corn, every man for his own particular, and in that regard trust to themselves; in all other things to go on in the general way as before. And so [was] assigned to every family a parcel of land, according to the proportion of their number for that end, only for present use (but made no division for inheritance), and ranged all boys and youth under some family. This had very good success, for it made all hands very industrious, so as much more corn was planted than otherwise would have been by any means the governor or any other could use, and saved him a great deal of trouble and gave far better content. The women now went willingly into the field, and took their little ones with them to set corn, which before would allege weakness and inability, whom to have compelled would have been thought great tyranny and oppression.

The experience that was had in this common course and condition, tried sundry years and that among godly and sober men, may well evince the vanity of that conceit of Plato's and other ancients applauded by some of later times—that the taking away of property and bringing in community into a commonwealth would make them happy and flourishing, as if they were wiser than God. For this community (so far as it was)was found to breed much confusion and discontent and retard much employment that would have been to their benefit and comfort. For the young men that were most able and fit for labor and service did repine that they should spend their time and strength to work for other men's wives and children without any recompense. The strong, or man of parts, had no more in division of victuals and clothes than he that was weak and not able to do a quarter the other could; this was thought injustice. The aged and graver men to be ranked and equalized in labors and victuals, clothes, etc., with the meaner and younger sort thought it some indignity and disrespect unto them. And for men's wives to be commanded to do service for other men, as dressing their meat, washing their clothes, etc., they deemed it a kind of slavery; neither could many husbands well brook it. Upon the point

all being to have alike, and all to do alike, they thought themselves in the like condition and one as good as another; and so, if it did not cut off those relations that God has set among men, yet it did at least much diminish and take off the mutual respects that should be preserved among them. And it would have been worse if they had been men of another condition. Let none object this is men's corruption, and nothing to the course itself. I answer, seeing all men have this corruption in them, God in His wisdom saw another course fitter for them.

SHORT RATIONS

But to return, After this course [was] settled, and by that their corn was planted, all their victuals were spent, and they were only to rest on God's Providence, at night, not many times knowing where to have a bit of anything the next day. And so, as one well observed, had need to pray that God would give them their daily bread, above all people in the world. Yet they bore these wants with great patience and alacrity of spirit, and that for so long a time as for the most part of two years....

But alas! These, when they had maize (that is, Indian corn) they thought it as good as a feast and wanted not only for five days together, but sometime two or three months together, and neither had bread nor any kind of corn....

They having but one boat left and she not overwell fitted, they were divided into several companies, six or seven to a gang or company, and so went out with a net they had bought to take bass and suchlike fish by course, every company knowing their turn. No sooner was the boat discharged of what she brought but the next company took her and went out with her. Neither did they return till they had caught something, though it were five or six days before, for they knew there was nothing at home, and to go home empty would be a great discouragement to the rest. Yea, they strive who should do best. If she stayed long or got little, then all went to seeking of shellfish, which at low water they dug out of the sands. And this was their living in the summertime, till God sent them better; and in winter they were helped with peanuts and fowl. Also in the summer they got now and then a deer, for one or two of the fittest was appointed to range the woods for that end, and what was got that way was divided among them....

The *Anne* and *Little James*

About fourteen days after, came in this ship, called the *Anne*, whereof Mr. William Peirce was master; and about a week or ten days after, came in the pinnace which, in foul weather, they lost at sea—a fine, new vessel of about forty-four ton [the *Little James*], which the company had built to stay in the country. They brought about sixty persons for the general, some of them being very useful persons and became good members to the body; and some were the wives and children of such as were here already. And some were so bad as they were fain to be at charge to send them home again the next year. Also, besides these, there came a company that did not belong to the general body but came on their particular [on their own] and were to have lands assigned them and be for themselves, yet to be subject to the general government; which caused some difference and disturbance among them, as will after appear....

More Semistarvation

These passengers, when they saw their low and poor condition ashore, were much daunted and dismayed, and according to their diverse humors were diversely affected. Some wished themselves in England again; others fell a-weeping, fancying their own misery in what they saw now in others; othersome pitying the distress they saw their friends had been long in and still were under. In a word, all were full of sadness. Only some of their old friends rejoiced to see them, and that it was no worse with them, for they could not expect it should be better, and now hoped they should enjoy better days together. And truly it was no marvel they should be thus affected, for they were in a very low condition; many were ragged in apparel and some little better than half-naked, though some that were well stored before were well enough in this regard. But for food they were all alike, save some that had got a few peas of the ship that was last here. The best dish they could present their friends with was a lobster or a piece of fish without bread or anything else but a cup of fair spring water. And the long continuance of this diet, and their labors abroad, had something abated the freshness of their former complexion; but God gave them health and strength in a good measure, and showed them by experience the truth of that word, "That man liveth not by bread only, but by every word that proceedeth out of the mouth of the Lord doth a man live" (Deut. 8:3)....

I may not here omit how, notwithstand-[ing] all their great pains and industry and the great hopes of a large crop, the Lord seemed to blast and take away the same, and to threaten further and more sore famine unto them. By a great drought which continued from the third week in May till about the middle of July, without any rain and with great heat for the most part, inso-much as the corn began to wither away though it was set with fish, the moisture whereof helped it much. Yet at length it began to languish sore, and some of the drier grounds were parched like withered hay, part whereof was never recovered. Upon which they set apart a solemn day of humiliation to seek the Lord by humble and fervent prayer in this great distress. And He was pleased to give them a gracious and speedy answer, both to their own and the Indians' admiration that lived among them. For all the morning and greatest part of the day, it was clear weather and very hot, and not a cloud or any sign of rain to be seen; yet toward evening it began to overcast, and shortly after to rain with such sweet and gentle showers as gave them cause of rejoicing and blessing God. It came

without either wind or thunder or any violence, and by degrees in that abundance as that the earth was thoroughly wet and soaked and therewith; which did so apparently revive and quicken the decayed corn and other fruits, as was wonderful to see, and made the Indians astonished to behold. And afterward the Lord sent them such seasonable showers, with interchange of fair warm weather as, through His blessing, caused a fruitful and liberal harvest, to their no small comfort and rejoicing. For which mercy, in time convenient, they also set apart a day of thanksgiving.

On the other hand, the old planters were afraid that their corn, when it was ripe, should be imparted to the newcomers, whose provisions which they brought with them they feared would fall short before the year went about, as indeed it did. They came to the governor and besought him that as it was before agreed that they should set corn for their particular (and accordingly they had taken extraordinary pains thereabout) that they might freely enjoy the same; and they would not have a bit of the victuals now come, but wait till harvest for their own and let the newcomers enjoy what they had brought. They would have none of it except they could purchase any of it of them by bargain or exchange. Their request was granted them, for it gave both sides good content; for the newcomers were as much afraid that the hungry planters would have eaten up the provisions brought, and they should have fallen into the like condition.

This ship was in a short time laden with clapboard by the help of many hands. Also they sent in her all the beaver and other furs they had, and Mr. Winslow was sent over with her to inform of all things and procure such things as were thought needful for their present condition. By this time harvest was come, and instead of famine now God gave them plenty, and the face of things was changed, to the rejoicing of the hearts of many, for which they blessed God. And the effect of their particular planting was well seen, for all had, one way and other, pretty well to bring the year about; and some of the abler sort and more industrious had to spare, and sell to others; so as any general want or famine has not been among them since to this day.

Agreement with Newcomers

Those that came on their particular looked for greater matters than they found or could attain unto, about building great houses and such pleasant situations for them as themselves had fancied; as if they would be great men and rich all of a sudden. But they proved castles in the air. These were the conditions agreed on between the colony and them.

- That the governor, in the name and with the consent of the company, does in all love and friendship receive and embrace them, and is to allot them competent places for habitations within the town. And promises to show

them all such other courtesies as shall be reasonable for them to desire or us to perform.

- That they on their parts be subject to all such laws and orders as are already made, or hereafter shall be, for the public good.
- That they be freed and exempt from the general employments of the said company (which their present condition of community requires) except common defense and such other employments as tend to the perpetual good of the colony.
- Toward the maintenance of government and public officers of the said colony, every male above the age of sixteen years shall pay a bushel of Indian wheat, or the worth of it, into the common store.
- That, according to the agreement the merchants made with them before they came, they are to be wholly debarred from all trade with the Indians, for all sorts of furs and suchlike commodities, till the time of the communality be ended. ...

PLAN OF CIVIL GOVERNMENT FOR PROVIDENCE (1640)

Source: *Historical Collections; Consisting of State Papers, and Other Authentic Documents; Intended as Materials for An History of the United States of America,*

Ebenezer Hazard, ed., Philadelphia, 1792–1794, I, pp. 464–466.

We, Robert Coles, Chad Browne, William Harris, and John Warner, being freely chosen by the consent of our loving friends and neighbors, the inhabitants of this town of Providence, having many differences among us, they being freely willing and also bound themselves to stand to our arbitration in all differences among us, to rest contented in our determination being so betrusted, we have seriously and carefully endeavored to weigh and consider all those differences being desirous to bring to unity and peace, although our abilities are far short in the due examination of such weighty things; yet, so far as we conceive in laying all things together, we have gone the fairest and the equalest way to produce our peace.

I. *Agreed.* We have with one consent agreed that in the parting those particular properties which some of our friends and neighbors have in Pawtuxet, from the general common of our town of Providence to run upon a straight line from a fresh spring being in the gulley, at the head of that cove running by that point of land called Saxafras unto the town of Mashipawog to an oak tree standing near unto the cornfield, being at this time the nearest cornfield unto Pawtuxet, the oak tree having four marks with an axe, till some other landmark be set for a certain bound. Also, we agree that if any meadow ground lying and joining to that meadow that borders upon the river of Pawtuxet come within the foresaid line, which will not come within a straight line from Long Cove to the marked tree, then for that meadow to belong to Pawtuxet, and so beyond the town of Mashipawog from the oak tree between the two fresh rivers Pawtuxet and Wanasquatucket of an even distance.

II. *Agreed.* We have with one consent agreed that for the disposing of those lands that shall be disposed belonging to this town of Providence to be in the whole inhabitants by the choice of five men for general disposal to be betrusted with disposal of lands and also of the town's stock, and all general things, and not to receive in any in six days as townsmen but first to give the inhabitants notice to consider if any have just cause to show against the receiving of him as you can apprehend, and to receive none but such as subscribe to this our determination. Also we agree that if any of our neighbors do apprehend himself wronged by these or any of these five disposers, that at the general town meeting he may have a trial.

Also we agree for the town to choose, besides the other five men, one or more to keep record of all things belonging to the town and lying in common.

We agree, as formerly has been the liberties of the town, so still, to hold forth liberty of conscience.

III. *Agreed.* That after many considerations and consultations of our own state and also of states abroad in way of government, we apprehend no way so suitable to our condition as government by way of arbitration. But if men agree themselves by arbitration, no state we know of disallows that, neither do we. But if men refuse that which is but common humanity between man and man, then, to compel such unreasonable persons to a reasonable way, we agree that the five disposers shall have power to compel him either to choose two men himself, or if he refuse; for them to choose two men to arbitrate his cause; and if these four men chosen by every party do end the cause, then to see their determination performed and the faultive to pay the arbitrators for their time spent in it. But if those four men do not end it, then for the five disposers to choose three men to put an end to it; and for the certainty hereof we agree the major part of the five disposers to choose the three men, and the major part of the three men to end the cause having power from the five disposers by a note under their hand to perform it; and the faultive not agreeing in the first to pay the charge of the last, and for the arbitrators to follow no employment till the causes be ended without consent of the whole that have to do with the cause.

Instance. In the first arbitration, the offender may offer reasonable terms of peace, and the offended may exact upon him and refuse and trouble men beyond reasonable satisfaction, so for the last arbitrators to judge where the fault was, in not agreeing in the first, to pay the charge of the last.

IV. *Agreed.* That if any person damnify any man, either in goods or good name, and the person offended follow not the cause upon the offender, that if any person give notice to the five disposers, they shall call the party delinquent to answer by arbitration.

Instance. Thus, if any person abuse another in person or goods, maybe for peace sake a man will at present put it up, and it may so be resolved to revenge; therefore, for the peace of the state, the disposers are to look to it in the first place.

V. *Agreed*, for all the whole inhabitants to combine ourselves to assist any man in the pursuit of any party delinquent, with all our best endeavors to attack him; but if any man raise a hubbub, and there be no just cause, then for the party that raised the hubbub to satisfy men for their time lost in it.

VI. *Agreed.* That if any man have a difference with any of the five disposers which cannot be deferred till general meeting of the town, then he may have the clerk call the town together at his — — — for a trial.

Instance. It may be a man may be to depart the land, or to a far part of the land, or his estate may lie upon a speedy trial, or the like case may fall out.

VII. *Agreed.* That the town, by the five men, shall give every man a deed of all his lands lying within the bounds of the plantation, to hold it by for after ages.

VIII. *Agreed.* That the five disposers shall from the date hereof meet every month-day upon general things and at the quarter-day to yield a new choice and give up their old accounts.

IX. *Agreed.* That the clerk shall call the five disposers together at the month-day and the general town together every quarter, to meet upon general occasions from the date hereof.

X. *Agreed.* That the clerk is to receive for every cause that comes to the town for a trial 4*d*; for making each deed; 12*d*; and to give up the book to the town at the year's end, and yield to a new choice.

XI. *Agreed.* That all acts of disposal on both sides to stand since the difference.

XII. *Agreed.* That every man that has not paid in his purchase money for his plantation shall make up his 10*s*. to be 30*s*., equal with the first purchasers; and for all that are received, townsmen hereafter to pay the like sum of money to the town stock.

These being those things we have generally concluded on, for our peace, we desiring our loving friends to receive as our absolute determination, laying ourselves down as subjects to it.

WILLIAM PENN: THE PEOPLE CALLED QUAKERS (1696)

Source: *The Select Works of William Penn*, 4th edition, London, 1825, Vol. III, pp. 473–512.

That which the people called Quakers lay down as a main fundamental in religion is this, "That God, through Christ, has placed a principle in every man to inform him of his duty, and to enable him to do it; and that those that live up to this principle are the people of God; and those that live in disobedience to it are not God's people, whatever name they may bear or profession they may make of religion." This is their ancient, first, and standing testimony; with this they began, and this they bore, and do bear, to the world.

By this principle they understand something that is divine; and though in man, yet not of man, but of God; and that it came from Him, and leads to Him all those that will be led by it.

There are diverse ways of speaking they have been led to use, by which they declare and express what this principle is, about which I think fit to precaution the reader; viz., they call it "the light of Christ within man," or, "light within," which is their ancient, and most general and familiar phrase, also the manifestation or appearance of Christ; the witness of God, the seed of God; the seed of the kingdom; wisdom, the word in the heart; the grace that appears to all men; the spirit given to every man to profit with; the truth in the inward parts; the spiritual leaven that leavens the whole lump of man — which are many of them figurative expressions, but all of them such as the Holy Ghost had used, and which will be used in this treatise, as they are most frequently in the writings and ministry of this people. But that this variety and manner of expression may not occasion any misapprehension or confusion in the understanding of the reader, I would have him know that they always mean by these terms, or denominations, not another but the same principle, before mentioned; which, as I said, though it be in man, is not of man but of God, and therefore divine; and one in itself, though diversely expressed by the holy men, according to the various manifestations and operations thereof.

It is to this principle of light, life, and grace that this people refer all; for they say it is the great agent in religion; that, without which, there is no conviction, so no conversion, or regeneration, and consequently no entering into the kingdom of God. That is to say, there can be no true sight of sin, nor sorrow for it, and therefore no forsaking or overcoming of it, or remission or justification from it. A necessary and powerful principle, indeed, when neither sanctification nor justification can be had without it. In short, there is no becoming virtuous, holy, and good without this principle; no acceptance with God, nor peace of soul, but through it. But, on the contrary, that the reason of so much irreligion among Christians, so much superstition instead of devotion, and so much profession without enjoyment, and so little heart reformation, is because people, in religion, overlook this principle and leave it behind them.

They will be religious without it and Christians without it, though this be the only means of making them so indeed. So natural is it to man, in his degenerate state, to prefer sacrifice before obedience, and to make prayers go for practice, and so flatter himself to hope by ceremonial and bodily service, to excuse himself with God from the stricter discipline of this principle in the soul, which leads man to take up the cross, deny himself, and do that which God requires of him. And that is every man's true religion, and every such man is truly religious; that is, he is holy, humble, patient, meek, merciful, just, kind, and charitable; which, they say, no man can make himself, but that this principle will make them all so that will embrace the convictions and teachings of it, being the root of all true religion in man, and the good seed from whence all good fruits proceed. To sum up what they say upon the nature and virtue of it, as contents of that which follows, they declare that this principle is, first, divine; second, universal; third, efficacious, in that it gives man:

- First, the knowledge of God, and of himself; and therein a sight of his duty and disobedience to it.
- Second, it begets a true sense and sorrow for sin in those that seriously regard the convictions of it.
- Third, it enables them to forsake sin, and sanctifies from it.
- Fourth, it applies God's mercies, in Christ, for the forgiveness of sins that are past, unto justification, upon such sincere repentance and obedience.
- Fifth, it gives, to the faithful, perseverance unto a perfect man, and the assurance of blessedness, world without end.

To the truth of all which, they call in a threefold evidence: First, the Scriptures, which give an ample witness, especially those of the New and better Testament. Second, the reasonableness of it in itself. And, last, a general experience, in great measure, but particularly their own, made credible by the good fruits they have brought forth, and the answer God has given to their ministry; which, to impartial observers, have commended the principle.

ANONYMOUS: OPPORTUNITIES FOR SETTLERS IN CAROLINA (1666)

Source: *Historical Collections of South Carolina: Embracing Many Rare and Valuable Pamphlets, and Other Documents, Relating to the History,* B.R. Carroll, ed., New York, 1836, Vol. II, pp. 10–18.

Carolina is a fair and spacious province on the continent of America. ... The land is of diverse sorts as in all countries of the world. That which lies near the sea is sandy and barren, but bears many tall trees, which make good timber for several uses; and this sandy ground is by experienced men thought to be one cause of the healthfulness of the place. But up the river about twenty or thirty mile[s], where they have made a town, called Charles Town, there is plenty of as rich ground as any in the world. ... The woods are stored with deer and wild turkeys, of a great magnitude, weighing many times above 50 lb. a piece, and of a more pleasant taste than in England, being in their proper climate; other sorts of beasts in the woods that are good for food, and also fowls, whose names are not known to them.

This is what they found naturally upon the place; but they have brought with them most sorts of seeds and roots of the Barbadoes which thrive [in] the most temperate clime ... and they have potatoes, and the other roots and herbs of Barbadoes growing and thriving with them; as also from Virginia, Bermuda, and New England, what they could afford. They have indigo, tobacco, very good, and cotton wool; lime trees, orange, lemon, and other fruit trees they brought, thrive exceedingly. They have two crops of Indian corn in one year, and great increase every crop. Apples, pears, and other English fruit grow there out of the planted kernels.

The marshes and meadows are very large, from 1,500 to 3,000 acres and upwards, and are excellent food for cattle, and will bear any grain being prepared. Some cattle, both great and small, will live well all the winter, and keep their fat without fodder; hogs find so much mast and other food in the woods that they want no other care than a swineherd to keep them from running wild. The meadows are very proper for rice, rapeseed, linseed, etc., and may many of them be made to overflow at pleasure with a small charge.

Here are as brave rivers as any in the world, stored with great abundance of sturgeon, salmon, bass, plaice, trout, and Spanish mackerel, with many other most pleasant sorts of fish, both flat and round, for which the English tongue has no name. Also, in the little winter they have, abundance of wild geese, ducks, teals, widgeons, and many other pleasant fowl. And (as it is said before) the rivers are very deep and navigable above 100 miles up; also there are wholesome springs and rivulets.

Last of all, the air comes to be considered, which is not the least considerable to the well being of a plantation, for without a wholesome air all other considerations avail nothing. And this is it which makes this place so desirable, being seated in the glorious light of heaven brings many advantages, and His convenient distance secures them from the inconvenience of His scorching beams. ...

If, therefore, any industrious and ingenious persons shall be willing to partake of the felicities of this country, let them embrace the first opportunity, that they may obtain the greater advantages.

The chief of the privileges are as follows:

- First, there is full and free liberty of conscience granted to all, so that no man is to be molested or called in question for matters of religious concern; but everyone to be obedient to the civil government, worshiping God after their own way.
- Second, there is freedom from custom for all wine, silk, raisins, currants, oil, olives, and almonds that shall be raised in the province for seven years, after four ton of any of those commodities shall be imported in one bottom.

- Third, every freeman and free-woman that transport themselves and servants by the 25th of March next, being 1667, shall have for himself, wife, children, and menservants, for each 100 acres of land for him and his heirs forever, and for every woman-servant and slave, 50 acres, paying at most ½d. per acre, per annum, in lieu of all demands, to the Lords Proprietors; provided always that every man be armed with a good musket full bore, 10 lb. powder, and 20 lb. of bullet, and six-months provision for all, to serve them while they raise provision in that country.
- Fourth, every manservant, at the expiration of their time, is to have of the country 100 acres of land to him and his heirs forever, paying only ½d. per acre, per annum, and the women, 50 acres of land on the same conditions; their masters also are to allow them two suits of apparel and tools such as he is best able to work with, according to the custom of the country.
- Fifth, they are to have a governor and council appointed from among themselves to see the laws of the Assembly put in due execution; but the governor is to rule but three years, and then learn to obey; also he has no power to lay any tax or make or abrogate any

law without the consent of the colony in their Assembly.

- Sixth, they are to choose annually from among themselves a certain number of men, according to their divisions, which constitute the General Assembly with the governor and his council, and have the sole power of making laws and laying taxes for the common good when need shall require.

These are the chief and fundamental privileges, but the Right Honorable Lords Proprietors have promised (and it is their interest so to do) to be ready to grant what other privileges may be found advantageous for the good of the colony.

Is there, therefore, any younger brother who is born of gentile blood, and whose spirit is elevated above the common sort, and yet the hard usage of our country has not allowed suitable fortune; he will not surely be afraid to leave his native soil to advance his fortunes equal to his blood and spirit, and so he will avoid these unlawful ways too many of our young gentlemen take to maintain themselves according to their high education, having but small estates. Here, with a few servants and a small stock, a great estate may be raised, although his birth have not entitled him to any of the land of his ancestors, yet his industry may supply him so, as to make him the head of as famous a family.

Such as are here tormented with much care how to get worth to gain a livelihood, or that with their labor can hardly get a comfortable subsistence, shall do well to go to this place, where any man whatever that is but willing to take moderate pains may be assured of a most comfortable subsistence, and be in a way to raise his fortunes far beyond what he could ever hope for in England. Let no man be troubles at the thoughts of being a servant for four or five years, for I can assure you that many men give money with their children to serve seven years, to take more pains and fare nothing so well as the servants in this plantation will do. Then, it is to be considered that so soon as he is out of his time, he has land and tools, and clothes given him, and is in a way of advancement.

Therefore, all artificers, as carpenters, wheelwrights, joiners, coopers, bricklayers, smiths, or diligent husbandmen and laborers that are willing to advance their fortunes and live in a most pleasant healthful and fruitful country, where artificers are of high esteem and used with all civility and courtesy imaginable, may take notice that there is an opportunity offered now by the Virginia Fleet, from whence Cape Fear is but three or four days' sail, and then a small stock carried to Virginia will purchase provisions at a far easier rate than to carry them from hence; also the freight of the said provisions will be saved, and be more fresh, and there wants not conveyance from Virginia thither.

If any maid or single woman have a desire to go over, they will think themselves in the Golden Age, when men paid a dowry for their wives; for if they be but civil, and under fifty years of age, some honest man or other will purchase them for their wives.

Those that desire further advice, or servants that would be entertained, let them repair to Mr. Matthew Wilkinson, ironmonger, at the sign of the Three Feathers in Bishopsgate Street, where they may be informed when the ships will be ready, and what they must carry with them.

PETER FONTAINE: A DEFENSE OF SLAVERY IN VIRGINIA (1757)

Source: *Memoirs of a Huguenot Family*, Ann Maury, ed., New York, 1853, pp. 348–353.

Now, to answer your first query — whether by our breach of treaties we have not justly exasperated the bordering nations of Indians against us, and drawn upon ourselves the barbarous usage we meet with from them and the French? To answer this fully would take up much time. I shall only hint at some things which we ought to have done, and which we did not do at our first settlement among them, and which we might have learned long since from the practice of our enemies the French.

I am persuaded we were not deficient in the observation of treaties, but, as we got the land by concession and not by conquest, we ought to have intermarried with them, which would have incorporated us with them effectually, and made of them staunch friends, and, which is of still more consequence, made many of them good Christians. But this our wise politicians at home put an effectual stop to at the beginning of our settlement here, for, when they heard that Rolfe had married Pocahontas, it was deliberated in Council whether he had not committed high treason by so doing, that is, marrying an Indian Princess. And had not some troubles intervened which put a stop to the inquiry, the poor man might have been hanged up for doing the most just, the most natural, the most generous and politic action that ever was done this side of the water. This put an effectual stop to all intermarriages afterward.

Our Indian traders have indeed their squaws, alias whores, at the Indian towns where they trade, but leave their offspring like bulls or boars to be provided for at random by their mothers. As might be expected, some of these bastards have been the leading men or war captains that have done us so much mischief. This ill treatment was sufficient to create jealousy in the natural man's breast, and made the Indians look upon us as false and deceitful friends, and cause all our endeavors to convert them to be ineffectual. But here, methinks, I can hear you observe — What! Englishmen intermarry with Indians? But I can convince you that they are guilty of much more heinous practices, more unjustifiable in the sight of God and man (if that, indeed, may be called a bad practice), for many base wretches among us take up with Negro women, by which means the country swarms with mulatto bastards, and these mulattoes, if but three generations removed from the black father or mother, may, by the indulgence of the laws of the country, intermarry with the white people, and actually do every day so marry.

Now, if, instead of this abominable practice which has polluted the blood of many among us, we had taken Indian wives in the first place, it would have made them some compensation for their lands. They are a free people, and the offspring would not be born in a state of slavery. We should become rightful heirs to their lands and should not have smutted our blood; for the Indian children when born are as white as Spaniards or Portuguese, and were it not for the practice of going naked in the summer and besmearing themselves with bears' grease, etc., they would continue white. And had we thought fit to make them our wives, they would readily have complied with our fashion of wearing clothes all the year round; and, by doing justice to these poor, benighted heathen, we should have introduced Christianity among them.

Your own reflections upon these hints will be a sufficient answer to your first query. I shall only add that General Johnson's success was owing, under God, to his fidelity to the Indians and his generous conduct to his Indian wife, by whom he has several hopeful sons, who are all war captains, the bulwarks with

him of the Five Nations, and loyal subjects to their mother country.

As to your second query, if enslaving our fellow creatures be a practice agreeable to Christianity, it is answered in a great measure in many treatises at home, to which I refer you. I shall only mention something of our present state here.

Like Adam, we are all apt to shift off the blame from ourselves and lay it upon others, how justly in our case you may judge. The Negroes are enslaved by the Negroes themselves before they are purchased by the masters of the ships who bring them here. It is, to be sure, at our choice whether we buy them or not, so this then is our crime, folly, or whatever you will please to call it.

But our Assembly, foreseeing the ill consequences of importing such numbers among us, has often attempted to lay a duty upon them which would amount to a prohibition, such as £ 10 or £ 20 a head; but no governor dare pass such a law, having instructions to the contrary from the Board of Trade at home. By this means they are forced upon us, whether we will or will not. This plainly shows the African Company has the advantage of the colonies, and may do as it pleases with the Ministry.

Indeed, since we have been exhausted of our little stock of cash by the war, the importation has stopped; our poverty then is our best security. There is no more picking for their ravenous jaws upon bare bones; but should we begin to thrive, they will be at the same again. All our taxes are now laid upon slaves and on shippers of tobacco, which they wink at while we are in danger of being torn from them, but we dare not do it in time of peace, it being looked upon as the highest presumption to lay any burden upon trade. This is our part of the grievance, but to live in Virginia without slaves is morally impossible.

Before our troubles, you could not hire a servant or slave for love or money, so that, unless robust enough to cut wood, to go to mill, to work at the hoe, etc., you must starve or board in some family where they both fleece and half starve you. There is no set price upon corn, wheat, and provisions; so they take advantage of the necessities of strangers, who are thus obliged to purchase some slaves and land. This, of course, draws us all into the original sin and curse of the country of purchasing slaves, and this is the reason we have no merchants, traders, or artificers of any sort but what become planters in a short time.

A common laborer, white or black, if you can be so much favored as to hire one, is 1s. sterling or 15d. currency per day; a bungling carpenter, 2s. or 2s. 6d. per day; besides diet and lodging. That is, for a lazy fellow to get wood and water, £ 19 16s. 3d. current per annum; add to this £ 7 or £ 8 more and you have a slave for life.

ROBERT BEVERLEY: LOW CHARACTER OF IMMIGRANTS TO VIRGINIA (1705)

Source: Excerpt from *The History and Present State of Virginia, In Four Parts*, London, 1705, Pt. 3, Chs. 15, 16.

I can easily imagine with Sir Josiah Child, that this, as well as all the rest of the plantations, was for the most part at first peopled by persons of low circumstances, and by such as were willing to seek their fortunes in a foreign country. Nor was it hardly possible it should be otherwise; for 'tis not likely that any man of a plentiful estate should voluntarily abandon a happy certainty to roam after imaginary advantages in a New World. Besides which uncertainty, he must have proposed to himself to encounter the infinite difficulties and dangers that attend a new settlement. These discouragements were sufficient to terrify any man that could live easy in England from going to provoke his fortune in a strange land.

Those that went over to that country first were chiefly single men, who had not the encumbrance of wives and children in England; and if they had, they did not expose them to the fatigue and hazard of so long a voyage, until they saw how it should fare with themselves. From hence it came to pass that, when they were settled there in a comfortable way of subsisting a family, they grew sensible of the misfortune of wanting wives, and such as had left wives in England sent for them; but the single men were put to their shifts. They excepted against the Indian women, on account of their being pagans, and for fear they should conspire with those of their own nation to destroy their husbands.

Under this difficulty they had no hopes but that the plenty in which they lived might invite modest women of small fortunes to go over thither from England. However, they would not receive any but such as could carry sufficient certificate of their modesty and good behavior. Those, if they were but moderately qualified in all other respects, might depend upon marrying very well in those days, without any fortune. Nay, the first planters were so far from expecting money with a woman that 'twas a common thing for them to buy a deserving wife at the price of £100 and make themselves believe they had a hopeful bargain.

But this way of peopling the colony was only at first; for after the advantages of the climate and the fruitfulness of the soil were well known, and all the dangers incident to infant settlements were over, people of better condition retired thither with their families, either to increase the estates they had before, or else to avoid being persecuted for their principles of religion or government.

Thus in the time of the Rebellion in England, several good Cavalier families went thither with their effects to escape the tyranny of the usurper. And so again, upon the Restoration, many people of the opposite party took refuge there, to shelter themselves from the King's resentment. But they had not many of these last, because that country was famous for holding out the longest for the royal family of any of the English dominions; for which reason, the Roundheads went for the most part to New England, as did most of those that in the reign of King Charles II were molested on the account of their religion, though some of

these fell likewise to the share of Virginia. As for malefactors condemned to transportation, they have always received very few, and for many years last past, their laws have been severe against them.

WILLIAM BYRD: SURVEYING THE FRONTIER (1728)

Source: Excerpt from *William Byrd's Histories of the Dividing Line Betwixt Virginia and North Carolina*, William K. Boyd, ed., Raleigh, 1929.

March 9. The surveyors entered early upon their business this morning and ran the line through Mr. Eyland's plantation, as far as the banks of North River. They passed over it in the pirogue and landed in Gibbs's marsh, which was a mile in breadth and tolerably firm. They trudged through this marsh without much difficulty as far as the highland, which promised more fertility than any they had seen in these parts. But this firm land lasted not long before they came upon the dreadful pocoson [swamp] they had been threatened with. Nor did they find it one jot better than it had been painted to them. The beavers and otters had rendered it quite impassable for any creature but themselves.

Our poor fellows had much ado to drag their legs after them in this quagmire, but, disdaining to be balked, they could hardly be persuaded from pressing forward by the surveyors, who found it absolutely necessary to make a traverse in the deepest place to prevent their sticking fast in the mire and becoming a certain prey to the turkey buzzards.

This horrible day's work ended two miles to the northward of Mr. Merchant's plantation, divided from Northwest River by a narrow swamp, which is causewayed over. We took up our quarters in the open field not far from the house, correcting, by a fire as large as a Roman funeral pile, the aguish exhalations arising from the sunken grounds that surrounded us.

The neck of land included between North River and Northwest River, with the adjacent marsh, belonged formerly to Governor Gibbs but, since his decease, to Colonel Bladen, in right of his first lady, who was Mr. Gibbs's daughter. It would be a valuable tract of land in any country but North Carolina, where, for want of navigation and commerce, the best estate affords little more than a coarse subsistence.

10. The Sabbath happened very opportunely to give some ease to our jaded people, who rested religiously from every work but that of cooking the kettle. We observed very few cornfields in our walks, and those very small, which seemed the stranger to us because we could see no other tokens of husbandry or improvement. But upon further inquiry, we were given to understand people only made corn for themselves and not for their stocks, which know very well how to get their own living. ...

The only business here is raising of hogs, which is managed with the least trouble and affords the diet they are most fond of. The truth of it is, the inhabitants of North Carolina devour so much swine's flesh that it fills them full of gross humors. For want, too, of a constant supply of salt, they are commonly obliged to eat it fresh, and that begets the highest taint of scurvy. Thus, whenever a severe cold happens to constitutions thus vitiated, 'tis apt to improve into the yaws, called there very justly the country distemper. This has all the symptoms of the pox, with this aggravation, that no preparation of mercury will touch it. First it seizes the throat, next the palate, and lastly shows its spite to the poor nose, of which 'tis apt in a small time treacherously to undermine the foundation.

11. We ordered the surveyors early to their business, who were blessed with pretty dry grounds for three miles together. But they paid dear for it in the next two, consisting of one continued frightful pocoson, which no creatures but those of the amphibious kind ever had ventured into before. This filthy quagmire did in earnest put the men's courage to a trial, and though I can't say it made them lose their patience. yet they lost their humor for joking. They kept their gravity like so many Spaniards, so that a man might then have taken his opportunity to plunge up to the chin without danger of being laughed at. However, this unusual composure of countenance could not fairly be called complaining.

Their day's work ended at the mouth of Northern's Creek, which empties itself into Northwest River; though we chose to quarter a little higher up the river, near Mossy Point. This we did for the convenience of an old house to shelter our persons and baggage from the rain, which threatened us hard. We judged the thing right, for there fell a heavy shower in the night that drove the most hardy of us into the house. Though indeed our case was not much mended by retreating thither, because that tenement having not long before been used as a pork store, the moisture of the air dissolved the salt that lay scattered on the floor, and made it as wet within doors as without. However, the swamps and marshes we were lately accustomed to had made such beavers and otters of us that nobody caught the least cold.

We had encamped so early that we found time in the evening to walk near half a mile into the woods. There we came upon a family of mulattoes that called themselves free, though by the shyness of the master of the house, who took care to keep least in sight, their freedom seemed a little doubtful. It is certain many slaves shelter themselves in this obscure part of the world, nor will any of their righteous neighbors discover them. On the contrary, they find their account in settling such fugitives on some out-of-the-way corner of their land to raise stocks for a mean and inconsiderable share, well knowing their condition makes it necessary for them to submit to any terms.

Nor were these worthy borderers content to shelter runaway slaves, but debtors and criminals have often met with the like indulgence. But if the government of North Carolina has encouraged this unneighborly policy in order to increase their people, it is no more than what ancient Rome did before them, which was made a city of refuge for all debtors and fugitives, and from that wretched beginning grew up in time to be mistress of a great part of the world. And considering how fortune delights in bringing great things out of small, who knows but Carolina may, one time or other, come to be the seat of some other great empire?...

16. The line was this day carried one mile and a half and sixteen poles. The soil continued soft and miry, but fuller of trees, especially white cedars. Many of these, too, were thrown down and piled in heaps, high enough for a good Muscovite fortification. The worst of it was the poor fellows began now to be troubled with fluxes, occasioned by had water and moist lodging, but chewing of rhubarb kept that malady within bounds. ...

We passed by no less than two Quaker meeting houses, one of which had an awkward ornament on the west end of it, that seemed to ape a steeple. I must own I expected no such piece of foppery from a sect of so much outside simplicity. That persuasion prevails much in the lower end of Nansemond County, for want of ministers to pilot the people a decenter way to heaven. The ill reputation of tobacco planted in those lower parishes makes the clergy unwilling to accept of them, unless it be such whose abilities are as mean as their pay. Thus, whether the churches be quite void or but indifferently filled, the Quakers will have an opportunity of gaining proselytes. 'Tis a wonder no popish missionaries are sent from Maryland to labor in this neglected vineyard, who we know have zeal enough to traverse sea and land on the meritorious errand of making converts.

Nor is it less strange that some wolf in sheep's clothing arrives not from New England to lead astray a flock that has no shepherd. People uninstructed in any religion are ready to embrace the first that offers. It is natural for helpless man to adore his Maker in some form or other, and were there any exception to this rule, I should suspect it to be among the Hottentots of the Cape of Good Hope and of North Carolina....

17. They were, however, forced to keep the Sabbath in spite of their teeth, contrary to the dispensation our good chaplain had given them. Indeed, their short allowance of provision would have justified their making the best of their way, without distinction of days. 'Twas certainly a work both of necessity and self-preservation to save themselves from starving. Nevertheless, the hard rain had made everything so thoroughly wet that it was quite impossible to do any business. They therefore made a virtue of what they could not help and contentedly rested in their dry situation.

Since the surveyors had entered the Dismal, they had laid eyes on no living creature: neither bird nor beast, insect nor reptile came in view. Doubtless the eternal shade that broods over this mighty bog and hinders the sunbeams from blessing the ground makes it an uncomfortable habitation for anything that has life. Not so much as a Zealand frog could endure so aguish a situation. It had one beauty, however, that delighted the eye, though at the expense of all the other senses: the moisture of the soil preserves a continual verdure and makes every plant an evergreen, but at the same time the foul damps ascend without ceasing, corrupt the air, and render it unfit for respiration. Not even a turkey buzzard will venture to fly over it, no more that the Italian vultures will over the filthy Lake Avernus, or the birds in the Holy Land over the Salt Sea where Sodom and Gomorrah formerly stood.

In these sad circumstances, the kindest thing we could do for our suffering friends was to give them a place in the litany. Our chaplain, for his part, did his office and rubbed us up with a seasonable sermon. This was quite a new thing to our brethren of North Carolina, who live in a climate where no clergyman can breathe any more than spiders in Ireland.

For want of men in holy orders, both the members of the council and justices of the peace are empowered by the laws of that country to marry all those who will not take one another's word; but for the ceremony of christening their children, they trust that to chance. If a parson come in their way, they will crave a cast of his office, as they call it, else they are content their offspring should remain as errant pagans as themselves. They account it among their greatest advantages that they are not priest-ridden, not remembering that the clergy is rarely guilty of bestriding such as have the misfortune to be poor.

One thing may be said for the inhabitants of that province, that they are not troubled with any religious fumes and have the least superstition of any people living. They do not know Sunday from any other day, any more than Robinson Crusoe did, which would give them a great advantage were they given to be industrious. But they keep so many Sabbaths every week that their disregard of the seventh day has no manner of cruelty in it, either to servants or cattle....

21. The surveyors and their attendants began...to be alarmed with apprehensions of famine....Their provisions were now near exhausted. They had this morning made the last distribution, that so each might husband his small pittance as he pleased. Now it was that the fresh colored young man began to tremble, every joint of him, having dreamed the night before that the Indians were about to barbecue him over live coals. The prospect of famine determined the people at last, with one consent, to abandon the line for the present, which advanced but slowly, and make the best of their way to firm land.

Accordingly, they set off very early, and, by the help of the compass which they carried along with them, steered a direct westwardly course. They marched from morning till night and computed their journey to amount to about four miles, which was a great way considering the difficulties of the ground. It was

all along a cedar swamp, so dirty and perplexed that, if they had not traveled for their lives they could not have reached so far. On their way they espied a turkey buzzard that flew prodigiously high to get above the noisome exhalations that ascend from that filthy place. This they were willing to understand as a good omen, according to the superstitions of the ancients, who had great faith in the flight of vultures. However, after all this tedious journey, they could yet discover no end of their toil, which made them very pensive, especially after they had eaten the last morsel of their provisions. But, to their unspeakable comfort, when all was hushed in the evening, they heard the cattle low and the dogs bark very distinctly, which, to men in that distress, was more delightful music than Faustina or Farinelli could have made. In the meantime the commissioners could get no news of them from any of their visitors, who assembled from every point of the compass....

22. Our patrol happened not to go far enough to the northward this morning; if they had, the people in the Dismal might have heard the report of their guns. For this reason they returned without any tidings, which threw us into a great though unnecessary perplexity. This was now the ninth day since they entered into that inhospitable swamp, and consequently we had reason to believe their provisions were quite spent. We knew they worked hard and therefore would eat heartily so long as they had wherewithal to recruit their spirits, not imagining the swamp so wide as they found it. Had we been able to guess where the line would come out, we would have sent men to meet them with a fresh supply; but as we could know nothing of that, and as we had neither compass nor surveyor to guide a messenger on such an errand, we were unwilling to expose him to no purpose; therefore, all we were able to do for them, in so great an extremity, was to recommend them to a merciful Providence.

However long we might think the time, yet we were cautious of showing our uneasiness, for fear of mortifying our landlord. He had done his best for us, and therefore we were unwilling he should think us dissatisfied with our entertainment. In the midst of our concern, we were most agreeably surprised, just after dinner, with the news that the Dismalites were all safe....

24. This being Sunday, we had a numerous congregation, which flocked to our quarters from all the adjacent country. The news that our surveyors were come out of the Dismal increased the number very much, because it would give them an opportunity of guessing, at least, whereabouts the line could cut, whereby they might form some judgment whether they belonged to Virginia or Carolina. Those who had taken up land within the disputed bounds were in great pain lest it should be found to lie in Virginia; because this being done contrary to an express order of that government, the patentees had great reason to fear they should in that case have lost

their land. But their apprehensions were now at an end when they understood that all the territory which had been controverted was like to be left in Carolina....

BENJAMIN FRANKLIN: THE SPEECH OF POLLY BAKER (1747)

Source: *The Writings of Benjamin Franklin*, Albert H. Smyth, ed., New York, 1905, Vol. II, pp. 463–467.

The speech of Miss Polly Baker before a Court of Judicature, at Connecticut near Boston in New England, where she was prosecuted the fifth time for having a bastard child.

"May it please the Honorable Bench to indulge me in a few words. I am a poor, unhappy woman, who have no money to fee lawyers to plead for me, being hard put to it to get a tolerable living. I shall not trouble Your Honors with long speeches; nor have I the presumption to expect that you may, by any means, be prevailed on to deviate in your sentence from the law in my favor. All I humbly hope is that Your Honors would charitably move the governor's goodness in my behalf, that my fine may be remitted.

"This is the fifth time, gentlemen, that I have been dragged before your Court on the same account; twice I have paid heavy fines, and twice have been brought to public punishment for want of money to pay these fines. This may have been agreeable to the laws, and I don't dispute it; but since laws are sometimes unreasonable in themselves, and therefore repealed, and others bear too hard on the subject in particular instances, and therefore there is left a power somewhere to dispense with the execution of them, I take the liberty to say that I think this law, by which I am punished, is both unreasonable in itself, and particularly severe with regard to me, who have always lived an inoffensive life in the neighborhood where I was born, and defy my enemies (if I have any) to say I ever wronged any man, woman, or child.

"Abstracted from the law, I cannot conceive (may it please Your Honors) what the nature of my offense is. I have brought five fine children into the world, at the risk of my life; I have maintained them well by my own industry, without burdening the township; and would have done it better if it had not been for the heavy charges and fines I have paid. Can it be a crime (in the nature of things, I mean) to add to the number of the King's subjects, in a new country that really wants people? I own it, I should think it a praiseworthy rather than a punishable action. I have debauched no other woman's husband, nor enticed any youth; these things I never was charged with; nor has anyone the least cause of complaint against me, unless, perhaps, the minister or justice, because I have had children without being married, by which they have missed a wedding fee. But can this be a fault of mine?

"I appeal to Your Honors. You are pleased to allow I don't want sense; but I must be stupefied to the last degree not to prefer the honorable state of wedlock to the condition I have lived in. I always was, and still am, willing to enter into it; and doubt not my behaving well in it, having all the industry, frugality, fertility, and skill in economy appertaining to a good wife's character. I defy any person to say I ever refused an offer of that sort. On the contrary, I readily consented to the only proposal of marriage that ever was made me, which was when I was a virgin; but, too easily confiding in the person's sincerity that made it, I unhappily lost my own honor by trusting to his; for he got me with child, and then forsook me.

"That very person you all know; he is now become a magistrate of this county; and I had hopes he would have appeared this day on the bench, and endeavored to moderate the Court in my favor; then I should have scorned to mention it; but I must now complain of it as unjust and unequal, that my betrayer and undoer, the first cause of all my faults and miscarriages (if they must be deemed such), should be advanced to honor and power in that government that punishes my misfortunes with stripes and infamy!

"I shall be told, 'tis like, that were there no act of Assembly in this case, the precepts of religion are violated by my transgressions. If mine is a religious offense, leave it to religious punishments. You have already excluded me from the comforts of your church communion. Is not that sufficient? You believe I have offended Heaven, and must suffer eternal fire. Will not that be sufficient? What need is there then of your additional fines and whipping? I own I do not think as you do, for, if I thought what you call a sin was really such, I would not presumptuously commit it. But how can it be believed that Heaven is angry at my having children, when to the little done by me toward it God has been pleased to add His divine skill and admirable workmanship in the formation of their bodies and crowned it by furnishing them with rational and immortal souls?

"Forgive me, gentlemen, if I talk a little extravagantly on these matters. I am no divine, but if you, gentlemen, must be making laws, do not turn natural and useful actions into crimes by your prohibitions; but take into your wise consideration the great and growing number of bachelors in the country, many of whom, from the mean fear of the expenses of a family, have never sincerely and honorably courted a woman in their lives; and, by their manner of living, leave unproduced (which is little better than murder) hundreds of their posterity to the thousandth generation. Is not this a greater offense against the public good than mine? Compel them, then, by law, either to marry, or to pay double the fine of fornication every year.

"What shall poor young women do, whom custom has forbid to solicit the men, and who cannot force themselves upon husbands, when the laws take no care to provide them any, and yet severely punish them if they do their duty without them — the duty of the first great command of nature and of nature's God, 'increase and multiply'; a duty

from the steady performance of which nothing has been able to deter me. But for its sake I have hazarded the loss of the public esteem, and have frequently endured public disgrace; and therefore ought, in my humble opinion, instead of a whipping, to have a statue erected to my memory."

This judicious address influenced the Court to dispense with her punishment, and induced one of her judges to marry her the next day. She ever afterward supported an irreproachable character, and had fifteen children by her husband.

JOHN ELIOT: A COLLEGE PROPOSED FOR MASSACHUSETTS BAY (1633)

Source: Manuscript in the British Museum.

I earnestly desire that God will move your heart for the sake of the commonwealth, and also for the sake of learning (which I know you love and will be ready to further; indeed, we want a store of men to further that, for if we do not nourish learning, both church and commonwealth will sink). Because I am on this point, I beseech you to let me be bold enough to make one motion, for the furtherance of learning among us.

God has bestowed upon you a bountiful blessing, and if you should please to employ one mite of that great wealth which God has given, to erect a school of learning—a college—among us, you would be doing a glorious work, acceptable to God and man, and the commemoration of the first founder of the means of learning would perpetuate your name and honor among us.

Now, because my proposition may seem to require great costs, I will be bold to propose a way that will make it attainable with little.

First, there are no improved lands and revenues at present to maintain such a work. All the charge is the building of such a place as may be fit for such a purpose. And such learned men as are here and may come must, of their own proper charge, frequent those places at fit seasons, for the exercising of learning; and such young men as may be trained must bear their own costs.

We only want a convenient house. Now, the bare building of a house big enough for our young beginnings will be done with little cost. I doubt not that if you should set apart but £ 500 for that work it would be a sufficient beginning and would make convenient housing for the many years. Nay, £ 400 or £ 300 would do pretty well. And you would have this privilege: You should not need to send beforehand (if you should come) to build a house for your habitation for that would be ready to give you complete comfort....

For a library, and a place for the exercise of learning, it is my earnest desire and prayer that God would stir up the hearts of some well-wishers to learning to make such a beginning. Indeed, sir, I know of no one in every way more fitting than yourself. I beseech you, therefore, to consider it and to do that which may comfort

us. A library is the first project, and then a college. I know from our experience that we shall most need convenient chambers to entertain students, and a little room, which, I fear, will hold all of our first stock of books; then as they increase we may enlarge the room.

In our young beginnings, men lack funds for such buildings, and, therefore, public exercises of learning have not yet begun, though we have many learned men, both gentlemen and ministers. But if we had a suitable place we could have debates and lectures not only in divinity but in other arts and sciences and also in law, which is very important for the welfare of our commonwealth.

Now I will say no more, but will pray that the Lord will move your heart (which I hope is already moved) to be the first founder of so glorious a work as this.

PETER BULKELEY: A CITY SET UPON A HILL (1651)

Source: *The Gospel-Covenant; or The Covenant of Grace Opened*, 2nd edition, London, 1651, pp. 431–432.

Consider a time of separation must come wherein the Lord Jesus will divide and separate the holy from the unholy, as a shepherd separates the sheep from the goats. It will be good to be found among the saints at that day, and to stand in the assembly of the righteous. Woe, then, unto all those that are secluded from them, to all those that must stand without and be among dogs and devils, having no fellowship with Christ nor with his saints. It is good, therefore, to be holy. It will be found so then; woe unto the profane and ungodly at that day.

And for ourselves here, the people of New England, we should in a special manner labor to shine forth in holiness above other people. We have that plenty and abundance of ordinances and means of grace, as few people enjoy the like; we are as a city set upon a hill, in the open view of all the earth, the eyes of the world are upon us, because we profess ourselves to be a people in covenant with God, and therefore not only the Lord our God, with whom we have made covenant, but heaven and earth, angels and men, that are witnesses of our profession, will cry shame upon us if we walk contrary to the covenant which we have professed and promised to walk in. If we open the mouths of men against our profession, by reason of the scandalousness of our lives, we (of all men) shall have the greater sin....

Let us study so to walk that this may be our excellency and dignity among the nations of the world among which we live; that they may be constrained to say of us, only this people is wise, a holy and blessed people; that all that see us may see and know that the name of the Lord is called upon us; and that we are the seed which the Lord hath blessed (Deut. 28:10; Isa. 61:9).

There is no people but will strive to excel in something. What can we excel in, if not in holiness? If we look to number, we are the fewest; if to strength, we are the weakest; if to wealth and riches, we are the poorest of all the people of God through the whole world. We cannot excel (nor so much as equal) other people in these things; and if we come short in grace and holiness, too, we are the most despicable people under heaven; our worldly dignity is gone. If we lose the glory of grace, too, then is the glory wholly departed from our Israel, and we are become vile. Strive we, therefore, herein to excel, and suffer not this crown to be taken away from us. Be we a holy people, so shall we be honorable before God and precious in the eyes of His saints.

JONATHAN EDWARDS: ON THE GREAT RELIGIOUS REVIVAL (1743)

Source: *The Christian History, Containing Accounts of the Revival*, Boston, January 14, 21, 28, 1743/4.

Ever since the great work of God that was wrought here about nine years ago, there has been a great abiding alteration in this town in many respects. There has been vastly more religion kept up in the town, among all sorts of persons, in religious exercises and in common conversation than used to be before. There has remained a more general seriousness and decency in attending the public worship. There has been a very great alteration among the youth of the town with respect to reveling, frolicking, profane and unclean conversation, and lewd songs. Instances of fornication have been very rare. There has also been a great alteration among both old and young with respect to tavern haunting. I suppose the town has been in no measure so free of vice in these respects for any long time together for this sixty years as it has been this nine years past.

There has also been an evident alteration with respect to a charitable spirit to the poor (though I think with regard to this we in this town, as the land in general, come far short of Gospel rules). And though after that great work nine years ago there has been a very lamentable decay of religious affections and the engagedness of people's spirit in religion, yet many societies for prayer and social religion were all along kept up; and there were some few instances of awakening and deep concern about the things of another world, even in the most dead time.

In the year 1740, in the spring, before Mr. Whitefield came to this town, there was a visible alteration. There was more seriousness and religious conversation, especially among young people; those things that were of ill tendency among them were more forborne. And it was a more frequent thing for persons to visit their minister upon soul accounts; and in some particular persons there appeared a great alteration about that time. And thus it continued till Mr. Whitefield came to town, which was about the middle of October following. He preached here four sermons in the meeting-house (besides a private lecture at my house) — one on Friday, another on Saturday, and two upon the Sabbath. The congregation was extraordinarily melted by every sermon; almost the whole assembly being in tears for a great part of sermon time. Mr. Whitefield's sermons were suitable to the circumstances of the town, containing just reproofs of our backslidings, and, in a most moving and affecting manner, making use of our great profession and great mercies as arguments with us to return to God, from whom we had departed.

Immediately after this, the minds of the people in general appeared more engaged in religion, showing a greater forwardness to make religion the subject of their conversation, and to meet frequently together for religious purposes, and to embrace all opportunities to hear the Word preached. The revival at first appeared chiefly among professors and those that had entertained the hope that they were in a state of grace, to whom Mr. Whitefield chiefly addressed himself. But in a very short time there appeared an awakening and deep concern among some young persons that looked upon themselves as in a Christless state; and there were some hopeful appearances of conversion; and some professors were greatly revived.

In about a month or six weeks, there was a great alteration in the town, both as to the revivals of professors and awakenings of others. By the middle of December, a very considerable work of God appeared among those that were very young; and the revival of religion continued to increase; so that in the spring an engagedness of spirit about things of religion was become very general among young people and children, and religious subjects almost wholly took up their conversation when they were together.

In the month of May 1741, a sermon was preached to a company at a private house. Near the conclusion of the exercise, one or two persons that were professors were so greatly affected with a sense of the greatness and glory of divine things, and the infinite importance of the things of eternity, that they were not able to conceal it; the affection of their minds overcoming their strength, and having a very visible effect on their bodies. When the exercise was over, the young people that were present removed into the other room for religious conference; and particularly that they might have opportunity to inquire of those that were thus affected what apprehensions they had, and what things they were that thus deeply impressed their minds. And there soon appeared a very great effect of their conversation; the affection was quickly propagated through the room; many of the young people and children that were professors appeared to be overcome with a sense of the greatness and glory of divine things, and with admiration, love, joy and praise, and compassion to others that looked upon themselves as in a state of nature. And many others at the same time were overcome with distress about their sinful and miserable state and condition; so that the whole room was full of nothing but outcries, faintings, and suchlike.

Others soon heard of it, in several parts of the town, and came to them;

and what they saw and heard there was greatly affecting to them; so that many of them were overpowered in like manner. And it continued thus for some hours, the time spent in prayer, singing, counseling, and conferring. There seemed to be a consequent happy effect of that meeting to several particular persons, and in the state of religion in the town in general. After this were meetings from time to time attended with like appearances.

But a little after it, at the conclusion of the public exercise on the Sabbath, I appointed the children that were under sixteen years of age to go from the meetinghouse to a neighbor house, that I there might further enforce what they had heard in public, and might give in some counsels proper for their age. The children were there very generally and greatly affected with the warnings and counsels that were given them, and many exceedingly overcome; and the room was filled with cries. And when they were dismissed, they, almost all of them, went home crying aloud through the streets, to all parts of the town. The like appearances attended several such meetings of children that were appointed.

But their affections appeared by what followed to be of a very different nature; in many they appeared to be indeed but childish affections, and in a day or two would leave them as they were before. Others were deeply impressed; their convictions took fast hold of them and abode by them. And there were some that from one meeting to another seemed extraordinarily affected for some time, to but little purpose, their affections presently vanishing, from time to time; but yet afterward were seized with abiding convictions, and their affections became durable.

About the middle of the summer, I called together the young people that were communicants, from sixteen to twenty-six years of age, to my house; which proved to be a most happy meeting. Many seemed to be very greatly and most agreeably affected with those views which excited humility, self-condemnation, self-abhorrence, love, and joy; many fainted under these affections. We had several meetings that summer of young people attended with like appearances. It was about that time that there first began to be cryings out in the meetinghouse; which several times occasioned many of the congregation to stay in the house, after the public exercise was over, to confer with those who seemed to be overcome with religious convictions and affections; which was found to tend much to the propagation of their impressions, with lasting effect upon many, conference being at these times commonly joined with prayer and singing. In the summer and fall, the children in various parts of the town had religious meetings by themselves for prayer, sometimes joined with fasting; wherein many of them seemed to be greatly and properly affected, and I hope some of them savingly wrought upon.

The months of August and September were the most remarkable of any this year, for appearances of conviction and conversion of sinners, and great revivings, quickenings, and comforts of professors, and for extraordinary external effects of these things. It was a very frequent thing to see a houseful of outcries, faintings, convulsions, and suchlike, both with distress and also with admiration and joy. It was not the manner here to hold meetings all night, as in some places, nor was it common to continue them until very late in the night; but it was pretty often so that there were some that were so affected, and their bodies so overcome, that they could not go home, but were obliged to stay all night at the house where they were. There was no difference that I know of here, with regard to these extraordinary effects, in meetings in the night and in the daytime. The meetings in which these effects appeared in the evening, being commonly begun, and their extraordinary effects, in the day, and continued in the evening; and some meetings have been very remarkable for such extraordinary effects that were both begun and finished in the daytime.

There was an appearance of a glorious progress of the work of God upon the hearts of sinners in conviction and conversion this summer and fall; and great numbers. I think we have reason to hope, were brought savingly home to Christ. But this was remarkable, the work of God in His influences of this nature seemed to be almost wholly upon a new generation; those that were not come to years of discretion in that wonderful season nine years ago, children, or those that were then children. Others that had enjoyed that former glorious opportunity without any appearance of saving benefit seemed now to be almost wholly passed over and let alone. But now we had the most wonderful work among children that ever was in Northampton. The former great outpouring of the spirit was remarkable for influences upon the minds of children, beyond all that had ever been before; but this far exceeded that.

Indeed, as to influences on the minds of professors, this work was by no means confined to a new generation. Many of all ages partook of it; but, yet, in this respect, it was more general on those that were of the younger sort. Many that had formerly been wrought upon, that in the times of our declension had fallen into decays, and had in a great measure left God and gone after the world, now passed under a very remarkable new work of the spirit of God, as if they had been the subjects of a second conversion. They were first led into the wilderness, and had a work of conviction, having much greater convictions of the sin of both nature and practice than ever before (though with some new circumstances, and something new in the kind of conviction) in some with great distress, beyond what they had felt before their first conversion.

Under these convictions they were excited to strive for salvation, and the Kingdom of Heaven suffered violence from some of them in a far more remarkable manner than before. And after great convictions and humblings and agonizings with God, they had Christ discovered to them anew, as an All-sufficient Savior, and in the glories of His grace, and in a far more clear manner than before; and with greater humility, self-emptiness, and brokenness of heart, and a purer and higher joy, and greater desires after holiness of life, but with greater self-diffidence and distrust of their treacherous hearts.

One circumstance wherein this work differed from that which had been in the town five or six years before was that conversions were frequently wrought more sensibly and visibly; the impressions stronger and more manifest by external effects of them; and the progress of the spirit of God in conviction, from step to step, more apparent; and the transition from one state to another more sensible and plain; so that it might, in many instances, be as it were seen by by-standers. The preceding season had been very remarkable on this account beyond what had been before; but this more remarkable than that. And in this season these apparent or visible conversions (if I may so call them) were more frequently in the presence of others, at religious meetings, where the appearances of what was wrought on the heart fell under public observation....

In the beginning of the summer 1742, there seemed to be some abatement of the liveliness of people's affections in religion; but yet many were often in a great height of them. And in the fall and winter following, there were at times extraordinary appearances. But in the general, people's engagedness in religion and the liveliness of their affections have been on the decline; and some of the young people, especially, have shamefully lost their liveliness and vigor in religion, and much of the seriousness and solemnity of their spirits. But there are many that walk as becomes saints; and, to this day, there are a considerable number in the town that seem to be near to God, and maintain much of the life of religion, and enjoy many of the sensible tokens and fruits of His gracious presence.

With respect to the late season of revival of religion among us for three or four years past, it has been observable that in the former part of it, in the years 1740 and 1741, the work seemed to be much more pure, having less of a corrupt mixture, than in the former great outpouring of the spirit in 1735 and 1736. Persons seemed to be sensible of their former errors, and had learned more of their own hearts, and experience had taught them more of the tendency and consequences of things. They were now better guarded, and their affections were not only greater but attended with greater solemnity, and greater humility and self-distrust, and greater engagedness after holy living and perseverance; and there were fewer errors in conduct.

But in the latter part of it, in the year 1742, it was otherwise. The work continued more pure, till we were infected from abroad. Our people, hearing and some of them seeing the work in other places where there was a greater visible commotion than here, and the outward appearances were more extraordinary, were ready to think that the work in those places far excelled what was among us; and their eyes were dazzled with the high profession and great show that some made who came hither from other places.

That those people went so far beyond them in raptures and violent emotions of the affections and a vehement zeal, and what they called boldness for Christ, our people were ready to think was owing to their far greater attainments in grace and intimacy with Heaven. They looked little in their own eyes in comparison of them, and were ready to submit themselves to them, and yield themselves up to their conduct, taking it for granted that everything was right that they said and did. These things had a strange influence on the people, and gave many of them a deep and unhappy tincture, that it was a hard and long labor to deliver them from and which some of them are not fully delivered from to this day.

The effects and consequences of things among us plainly shows the following things, viz.: that the degree of grace is by no means to be judged of by the degree of joy, or the degree of zeal; and that indeed we cannot at all determine by these things who are gracious and who are not; and that it is not the degree of religious affections but the nature of them that is chiefly to be looked at. Some that have had very great raptures of joy, and have been extraordinarily filled (as the vulgar phrase is), and have had their bodies overcome, and that very often have manifested far less of the temper of Christians in their conduct since than some others that have been still and have made no great outward show. But then again there are many others that have had extraordinary joys and emotions of mind, with frequent great effects on their bodies, that behave themselves steadfastly as humble, amiable, eminent Christians.

'Tis evident that there may be great religious affections that may, in show and appearance, imitate gracious affections, and have the same effects on their bodies, but are far from having the same effect in the temper of their minds and course of their lives. And likewise there is nothing more manifest by what appears among us than that the goodness of persons' state is not chiefly to be judged of by any exactness of steps and method of experiences in what is supposed to be the first conversion; but that we must judge more by the spirit that breathes, the effect wrought on the temper of the soul, in the time of the work, and remaining afterward.

Though there have been very few instances among professors among us of what is ordinarily called scandalous sin known to me, yet the temper that some of them show and the behavior they have been of, together with some things in the kind and circumstances of their experiences, make me much afraid lest there be a considerable number that have woefully deceived themselves. Though, on the other hand, there is a great number whose temper and conversation is such as justly confirms the charity of others

toward them; and not a few in whose disposition and walk there are amiable appearances of eminent grace. And notwithstanding all the corrupt mixtures that have been in the late work here, there are not only many blessed fruits of it in particular persons that yet remain, but some good effects of it upon the town in general.

A party spirit has more ceased. I suppose there has been less appearance these three or four years past of that division of the town into two parties, that has long been our bane, than has been these thirty years. And the people have apparently had much more caution and a greater guard on their spirit and their tongues to avoid contention and unchristian heats in town meetings and on other occasions. And 'tis a thing greatly to be rejoiced in, that the people very lately have come to an agreement and final issue with respect to their grand controversy relating to their common lands; which has been above any other particular thing a source of mutual prejudices, jealousies, and debates for fifteen or sixteen years past.

The people are also generally of late in some respects considerably altered and meliorated in their notions of religion, particularly they seem to be much more sensible of the danger of resting in old experiences, or what they were subjects of at their supposed first conversion; and to be more fully convinced of the necessity of forgetting the things that are behind and pressing forward, and maintaining earnest labor, watchfulness, and prayerfulness as long as they live.

SAMUEL SEWALL: ON ACCOMMODATING THE INDIANS (1700)

Source: *Collections, Massachusetts Historical Society,* Cambridge and Boston, 1795, 6th series, I, pp. 231–233.

Last fall, I had notice of my being entrusted with a share in managing the Indian affairs, and presently upon it, the Commissioners were pleased to appoint me their secretary. As I account it an honor to be thus employed, so according to my mean ability, I shall endeavor faithfully to serve the Corporation and Commissioners, as I shall receive instructions from them.

I have met with an observation of some grave divines, that ordinarily when God intends good to a nation, He is pleased to make use of some of themselves to be instrumental in conveying of that good unto them. Now God has furnished several of the Indians with considerable abilities for the work of the ministry, and teaching school. And therefore I am apt to believe that if the Indians so qualified were more taken notice of in suitable rewards, it would conduce very much to the propagation of the Gospel among them. Besides the content they might have in a provision of necessary food and raiment, the respect and honor of it would quicken their industry and allure others to take pains in fitting themselves for a fruitful discharge of those offices.

One thing more I would crave leave to suggest. We have had a very long and grievous war with the Eastern Indians, and it is of great concernment to His Majesty's interests here that a peace be concluded with them upon firm and sure foundations; which in my poor opinion cannot well be while our articles of accord with them remain so very general as they do. I should think it requisite that convenient tracts of land should be set out to them; and that by plain and natural boundaries, as much as may be — as lakes, rivers, mountains, rocks — upon which for any Englishman to encroach should be accounted a crime. Except this be done, I fear their own jealousies, and the French friars, will persuade them that the English, as they increase and think they want more room, will never leave till they have crowded them quite out of all their lands. And it will be a vain attempt for us to offer Heaven to them if they take up prejudices against us, as if we did grudge them a living upon their own earth.

The Savoy Confession of Faith, English on one side and Indian on the other, has been lately printed here; as also several sermons of the president's [of Harvard, Increase Mather] have been transcribed into Indian and printed; which I hope in God's time will have a very good effect. To see it and be employed in giving Your Honor an account of it would be a very desirable piece of service to [me].

GLOSSARY

arable Fertile land that can be used for growing crops.

beachhead An area on a hostile shore occupied to secure further landing of troops and supplies.

charter A written agreement or contract that all parties must adhere to.

de facto Existing as a matter of course, without lawful authority.

dominion A self-governing nation of the British Commonwealth of Nations that acknowledges the British monarch as chief of state.

encroachment The state of advancing beyond reasonable, typical, or proper limits.

freemen People (typically men in colonial America) who are granted full civil and political rights as citizens.

immigrate To travel to a country of which one is not a native for permanent residence.

impecunious Habitually having very little or no money.

indentured The state of being contractually bound in service to another.

maize The American Indian word for corn.

metaphysics The philosophical study of the ultimate nature of reality.

oligarchic Pertaining to an oligarchy, which is government controlled by a small group.

omnipotence Having unlimited power and authority.

papist One who holds religious allegiance to the pope; sometimes used as a derogatory term for Roman Catholics.

proprietary Pertaining to the rights of ownership.

redemptioners Immigrants to America in the 18th and 19th centuries who obtained passage by becoming indentured servants.

squatter One who claims ownership of land merely by settling and working it, without title or payment of rent.

subsidy A grant by a government to a private person or company to assist an enterprise deemed advantageous to the public.

subsistence The minimum of food and shelter necessary to support life.

syncretism When multiple traditions, beliefs, and practices are fused into one.

travois A mode of transport consisting of two joined poles and a platform attached to both and draped between them that is dragged, most often by a horse or dog.

BIBLIOGRAPHY

DISCOVERY AND EXPLORATION

Useful introductions include Samuel Eliot Morison, *The European Discovery of America*, 2 vol. (1971–74); and David B. Quinn, *North America from Earliest Discovery to First Settlements: The Norse Voyages to 1612* (1977).

COLONIAL DEVELOPMENT TO 1763

OVERVIEWS

Charles M. Andrews, *The Colonial Period of American History*, 4 vol. (1934–38, reprinted 1964), is the starting point for an understanding of the structure of the British Empire in America. Lawrence Henry Gipson, *The British Empire Before the American Revolution*, 15 vol. (1936–70), represents the culmination of the "British Imperial" school of interpretation. Colin G. Calloway, *New Worlds for All: Indians, Europeans, and the Remaking of Early America* (1997); Peter Charles Hoffer, *The Brave New World: A History of Early America*, 2nd ed. (2006); Bernard Bailyn, *The Peopling of British North America: An Introduction* (1988); Gary B. Nash, *Red, White, and Black: The Peoples of Early America*, 6th ed. (2010); and Jack P. Greene and J.R. Pole (eds.), *Colonial British America* (1984), are excellent surveys.

SETTLEMENT

Perry Miller, *The New England Mind: The Seventeenth Century* (1939, reissued 1983), and a sequel, *The New England Mind: From Colony to Province* (1953, reissued 1967), together constitute perhaps the finest work of intellectual history ever written by an American historian. Francis Jennings, *The Invasion of America* (1975); James Axtell, *The European and the Indian* (1982), and Daniel Richter, *Facing East from Indian Country: A Native History of Early America* (2001), are important accounts of European-Indian relations. Edmund Morgan, *American Slavery, American Freedom: The Ordeal of Colonial Virginia* (2003); and *T.H. Breen* and *Stephen Innes*, *"Myne Owne Ground": Race and Freedom on Virginia's Eastern Shore, 1640-1676*, 25th anniversary ed. (2005), consider slavery and the African experience in colonial America.

IMPERIAL ORGANIZATION

Useful surveys include John Huxtable Elliott, *Empires of the Atlantic World: Britain and Spain in America, 1492–1830* (2006); Michael Kammen, *Empire and Interest: The American Colonies and the Politics of Mercantilism* (1970); and Stephen Saunders Webb, *1676, the End of American Independence* (1984).

THE GROWTH OF PROVINCIAL POWER

James A. Henretta, *The Evolution of American Society, 1700–1815* (1973), is an excellent survey of the American economic and political order. Jack P. Greene, *Pursuits of Happiness* (1988), seeks to demonstrate the variety of colonial social developments. Carl Bridenbaugh, *Myths and Realities: Societies of the Colonial South* (1952, reprinted 1981), argues persuasively that the colonial South consisted of not one but three sections. Rhys Isaac, *The Transformation of Virginia, 1740–1790* (1982), imaginatively surveys the social order of 18th-century Virginia. Gary B. Nash, *The Urban Crucible: The Northern Seaports and the Origins of the American Revolution*, abridged ed. (1986), surveys the growth of American cities in the 18th century. John J. McCusker and Russell R. Menard, *The Economy of British America, 1607–1789* (1985), is a good survey.

CULTURAL AND RELIGIOUS DEVELOPMENT

Daniel J. Boorstin, *The Americans: The Colonial Experience* (1958, reissued 1988), gives a brilliant, if overstated, account of American uniqueness. Henry F. May, *The Enlightenment in America* (1976), provocatively examines American intellectual development. Francis J. Bremer, *The Puritan Experiment: New England Society from Bradford to Edwards* (1995), surveys Puritan life and thought. Also informative is Brooke Hindle, *The Pursuit of Science in Revolutionary America, 1735–1789* (1956, reprinted 1974). Alan Heimert, *Religion and the American Mind, from the Great Awakening to the Revolution* (1966) makes an important though polemical contribution to the understanding of the Great Awakening.

AMERICA, ENGLAND, AND THE WIDER WORLD

Overviews are found in Brendan McConville, *The King's Three Faces: The Rise and Fall of Royal America, 1688-1776* (2006); Francis Parkman, *A Half-Century of Conflict*, 2 vol. (1892, reprinted 1965); Howard H. Peckham, *The Colonial Wars, 1689–1762* (1964); and Alan Rogers, *Empire and Liberty: American Resistance to British Authority, 1755–1763* (1974).

INDEX